AF252002

Rapid Appraisal and Health Policy

Rapid Appraisal and Health Policy

Bie Nio Ong

Reader in Health Services Research
Centre for Health Planning and Management
Keele University, UK

CHAPMAN & HALL

London · Glasgow · Weinheim · New York · Tokyo · Melbourne · Madras

For Barry, with all my love

Published by Chapman & Hall, 2–6 Boundary Row, London SE1 8HN, UK

Chapman & Hall, 2–6 Boundary Row, London SE1 8HN, UK

Blackie Academic & Professional, Wester Cleddens Road, Bishopbriggs, Glasgow G64 2NZ, UK

Chapman & Hall GmbH, Pappelallee 3, 69469 Weinheim, Germany

Chapman & Hall USA, 115 Fifth Avenue, New York NY 10003, USA

Chapman & Hall Japan, ITP-Japan, Kyowa Building, 3F, 2-2-1 Hirakawacho, Chiyoda-ku, Tokyo 102, Japan

Chapman & Hall Australia, 102 Dodds Street, South Melbourne, Victoria 3205, Australia

Chapman & Hall India, R. Seshadri, 32 Second Main Road, CIT East, Madras 600 035, India

Distributed in the USA and Canada by Singular Publishing Group Inc., 4284 41st Street, San Diego, California 92105

First edition 1996

Typeset in 10/12pt Times by Saxon Graphics Ltd, Derby
Printed in Great Britain by St Edmundsbury Press, Bury St Edmunds

ISBN 0 412 62820 1   1 56593 736 8 (USA)

♾ Printed on acid-free text paper, manufactured in accordance with ANSI/NISO Z39.48-1992 (Permanence of Paper).

Contents

Preface

It seems a long time ago that Susan Rifkin and Hugh Annett came to do a Rapid Appraisal with a group of people in South Sefton, Liverpool. We worked together very well as a team drawn from different organizations and learned a lot about the local community, the method, and ourselves. Since then, similar journeys have been made with many other groups of people in the United Kingdom, and most of the way I have travelled with Gerry Humphris, who helped developing the method further and with whom I discussed many theoretical and practical issues. For me, the main attraction of Rapid Appraisal lies in its ability to marry the rhetoric of community involvement with the reality of health policy making. While ideologically many people believe that communities should be involved in policy decisions, most of us are struggling with putting it into practice, and actually affect health policy in any real sense. Of course, Rapid Appraisal operates at a relatively small scale level, yet, it poses some very fundamental questions about power, knowledge and the nature of health policy, which go beyond local communities. In this book, I want to address these questions, and the practical operation of the system. I hope it will be of interest to people who are thinking about health policy and those who are doing it.

Although the act of writing a book may be an individual one, the thinking behind it is very much a collective enterprise. The first people to thank are all those known and unknown to me in the various communities where I have worked; they have given me the benefit of the doubt, and actively participated in the process of research and implementation. Secondly, I am grateful to all the people (too numerous to mention) who initiated a Rapid Appraisal and asked me to work with them; I specially want to mention Patrick Naish. I thank my colleagues at the Centre for Health Planning and Management, who not only gave me space to write, but also had to do some of my jobs (not always the nicest ones), including reading parts of this book. In particular, Calum Paton and Marilyn James provided very needed advice. Barbara Goodenough was invaluable in protecting my writing time, and in helping to put the final manuscript together.

Barry Munslow urged me to write this book, and has helped me to clarify my often nebulous ideas. He also created the domestic peace which made it possible for me to sit in my study undisturbed trying to be creative. And, of course, Karl and Jade, who took my writing seriously and often put their own concerns on the back burner. Without these three lovely people nothing would have happened.

Of course, none of the above-mentioned can be held responsible for the final product, which in the end is mine alone.

Introduction

 1

This book has a dual purpose: it seeks to demonstrate the way in which the Rapid Appraisal methodology is linked to a number of contemporary theoretical debates about health policy, and it intends to provide guidance for the implementation of its methodological principles. These two aims are complementary because the historical and conceptual foundations of Rapid Appraisal have shaped it into a complex, but flexible methodology. Moreover, tracing through its evolution enables its limitations and pitfalls to be highlighted, and its particular strengths to be emphasized.

While policy-makers and planners in health search for the 'all-singing, all-dancing' approach in health needs assessment, the argument advanced here is that this is like looking for the Holy Grail, and a pragmatic and creative approach can offer a greater chance of success. Of course, researchers realize that no such perfect methodology exists, and this is borne out by the increasing body of literature proposing multi-method research. In parallel, a re-consideration of how knowledge is derived has been taking place, attempting to examine the application, and in this process uncovering the limitations of the so-called hard, quantitative methods such as statistics or experimental research. In the field of health and, in particular, when trying to understand the experience of health and illness, a sole reliance on quantitative designs leads to incomplete knowledge.

Kumar (1994) argues that Rapid Appraisal can be considered as originating from two different traditions, one of which is ethnomethodology. This paradigm has as its underlying premise that reality is multi-layered, depending on the conceptions, preferences and interests of those investigators constructing the different realities. Rapid Appraisal is then seen as a tool to articulate the perspectives of those who are often ignored and to establish their world view as a valid one.

The second paradigm is rooted within logical positivism which presumes that social phenomena exist in the minds of individuals, but also exist as objective social reality. According to Kumar, Rapid Appraisal seeks to discover and describe social phenomena and processes in order to systematically explain their causes, and thus Rapid Appraisal is just one of many types of data-gathering methods to achieve this objective.

Most Rapid Appraisals, however, fall within the first paradigm, and emphasize the reliance on qualitative methods in order to understand people's subjectivity. This gradual shift has been assisted by what Denzin and Lincoln (1994) call 'a quiet methodological revolution in the social sciences' where a critique of a world view dominated by the natural science paradigms is gathering pace. They argue that this has led to a growing interest in linking research to social change, and to a blurring of disciplinary boundaries. It is precisely at this juncture that the emergence of the Rapid Appraisal methodology can be located: it is concerned with change, or more precisely, with influencing health policy, and it takes a multi-disciplinary and holistic perspective on health.

This book intends to explore the roots of the Rapid Appraisal methodology as coming from anthropology, geography, politics, epidemiology and sociology, whilst also providing a critique of the shortcomings within those disciplines when applied to the fields of health, health policy and community involvement. In common with other traditions such as, for example, Marxism and the action–research stemming from them, Rapid Appraisal focuses on 'making a difference'. This is achieved through sound, scientifically-based research that informs policy frameworks and decision-making processes. Specifically, Rapid Appraisal seeks to directly link the people in power with communities, thus placing a second level type of questioning on the agenda: are organizations – and individuals within them – willing and able to share power, question their own professional expertise, and able to change priorities? These are very big questions, and have been addressed before, but within the context of Rapid Appraisal these issues are specifically related to assessing health needs and user involvement.

The agenda for this book is potentially huge, and could explore complex territories such as needs and outcome assessment, priority-setting and rationing, the nature of knowledge and, in particular, professional versus lay knowledge. Whilst a treatment of these areas is adjacent to the discussion of the theoretical foundations of Rapid Appraisal, a more selective approach is required in order to maintain clarity and purpose within this book. Thus, the remainder of this introductory chapter will set out the basic principles underlying Rapid Appraisal, and the key themes connected with it. The selection of these themes excludes others which are perhaps equally important, but the danger of over-simplification and superficiality is greater than that of narrowing the discussion to the in-depth treatment of a smaller number of issues.

WHAT IS RAPID APPRAISAL?

Rapid Appraisal is primarily a methodology which provides timely, relevant information to decision-makers on pressing issues they face in the project and programme setting (Kumar, 1994). Conway (1988) describes it as follows in a more detailed manner:

1. greater speed compared with conventional methods of analysis;
2. working in the 'field';
3. an emphasis on learning directly from local inhabitants;
4. a semi-structured, multi-disciplinary approach with room for flexibility and innovation;
5. an emphasis on producing timely insights, hypotheses or 'best bets' rather than final truths or fixed recommendations.

When used within a health context, the aims of Rapid Appraisal are to gain insight into a community's perspective on their priority needs, which provides a picture of the strength of feeling rather than the quantifiable magnitude of a particular problem. The emphasis placed on subjectivity is deliberately based upon the idea that when people feel strongly about a particular issue they want to act upon it. This is directly related to the ultimate purpose of Rapid Appraisal which is action for change, grounded in sound understanding of needs and priorities within.

Rapid Appraisals in health have predominantly been carried out in developing countries and have been well documented (for example, Hurtado, 1990; Scrimshaw and Gleason, 1992). The emphasis in the majority of documents has been on developing rapid assessment methods which provide a diagnosis of communities' perceptions on specific problems such as water, sanitation, nutrition and so on. The focus for many researchers is on the methodological re-tooling (Cernea, 1992) through fully engaging and utilizing community knowledge in order to change the development planning process and implementation at community level. This often leads to an eclectic mix of research approaches combining, for example, mapping exercises, matrix ranking and scoring, focus groups, time lines and trend analysis (Chambers, 1992).

It can be argued that this emphasis on diagnosis is essential for raising the awareness in policy-makers of the legitimacy and relevance of community knowledge, and that the success of many social and health programmes crucially depends on understanding where 'communities are at'. Within this context Rapid Appraisal is seen as an inductive approach which builds on the concept that systems are interactive and rapidly changing, with health and social systems being no exception. In a sense, Rapid Appraisal can be considered as a challenge to conventional approaches in development which are top-down and expert-led.

One of the criticisms of Rapid Appraisal has been that it is transitory precisely because of its rapid nature, and that influencing policy cannot be sustained beyond a specific project. In the adaptations of Rapid Appraisal in the developed world this criticism has been taken on board, and consideration is given as to how communities can use Rapid Appraisal as a catalyst to get more embedded in the policy processes and exert influence in the longer term. This linkage between accessing community knowledge and incorporating this knowledge in decision-making (without losing its power to challenge) will be discussed in more detail in Chapter 5.

The important question is thus how Rapid Appraisal can make a difference at the level of leadership. The World Health Organization has argued that leadership should be people-centred (WHO, 1988a) and has to be built upon a sound understanding of people's needs in order to create and continue to progress a vision of health. Yet, it is uncommon for leaders to manage to stay in touch with the feelings of communities. A nationwide study in the United States has demonstrated the profound lack of confidence that Americans have in their leaders, both at national and local levels. Leaders fail to address issues that most concern the American public, notably in health, social issues and achieving a shared community vision. The survey reveals low levels of confidence in traditional local leaders in government, business and community, and leaders at state/federal and top government level are even less respected (ranging from 11–30% support). Their contribution to the improvement of health is considered low as they do not appear to understand communities' priorities (DYG Inc., 1994).

Comparing the experiences of communities in the developing and developed world reveals this gulf between those who make policy and those who are subject to the policy decisions. It is within this gap that approaches such as Rapid Appraisal attempt to operate and develop the methodologies through a theoretical analysis of key issues which bear upon the two pivots of leaders and communities. The remainder of this introductory chapter will outline the key theoretical considerations which are associated with Rapid Appraisal methodology and its implementation.

KEY THEMES

The broader context for Rapid Appraisal is the WHO 'Health for 2000' philosophy which has directed most of the work within the area of Primary Health Care around the globe (WHO, 1981). There has been considerable debate about the concept of Primary Health Care (PHC) – as opposed to Selective Primary

Health Care (SPHC) – which has been extensively appraised by Rifkin and Walt (1986). They argue that PHC is concerned with 'a development process by which people improve both their lives and life-styles' (p.560). As such PHC constitutes a strategy for health development and it places considerable emphasis on process and change.

Communities play an important role in both the process and in determining the direction of change, in particular, when addressing the issue of equity, the central pillar of PHC. Equity begs the question of the distribution of resources, and therefore requires a clear understanding of needs and priorities. Communities need to be in tandem with professionals and managers in this process in order to increase the understanding of the causes of ill-health and to effect possible solutions which help them to gain control over their present and future. Such dialogue and collaboration is aimed at achieving change which can be sustained through incremental improvements. Rifkin and Walt state very clearly that health improves as a result of continuous pressure on organizational structures and individual perspectives to move, and this does not always result in measurable outcomes, but rather offers a long-term vision. The linking of Rapid Appraisal with alternative visions of the future will be the subject of Chapter 8.

Taking the holistic definition of health by the WHO as a starting point Chapter 2 will review the implication of this definition on how health and health needs can be defined. This leads to a discussion of the limits to epidemiology which cannot take the experience of ill-health into account, and thus other disciplines have to illuminate this question. The cultural and social determinants of health and illness are important elements in the discussion, and flowing from there is the centrality of communities' own perceptions of health – its causality and the responses to ill-health. Rapid Appraisal recognizes the wider context of health and the way in which lay knowledge shapes perceptions and experiences of need. The specific question of how the concept of need converges or diverges with the growing market-orientation of public services in developed countries will be touched upon, as it sets structural limits to how needs are defined and whose perspectives count.

Chapter 3 continues to build on this theme by addressing the concept of community, which is central to Rapid Appraisal. It is recognized that this concept is far from unproblematic, and a review of current trends in the literature will be presented in order to examine what characterizes communities, how they function, what contribution they make to the health of individuals and related issues. While there is a long tradition of community development work, both in the developing world and in deprived urban areas of the developed world, relatively little research has been done on the interaction between community diagnosis and the policy process. The importance of joint diagnosis by communities and leaders in order to arrive at the formulation of needs and priorities will be discussed, and the distinction will be drawn between consultation and participation as consumer rights on the one hand, and advocacy and empowerment for citizens on the other hand. Rapid Appraisal adopts a particular and pragmatic interpretation of communities, and designs clear relationships between communities and leaders in order to achieve a common vision and agenda for action. Thus, it represents a move away from the consumer towards the citizen-based concept of involvement in policy.

This logically leads us to the broader question of power, its conceptual and political nature. Chapter 4 intends to engage in this discussion with particular reference to its application in health whilst drawing on some of the key theoretical debates surrounding the definition of power. The main focus will be on how power is exercised in determining health policy, and the role played by professionals – doctors, politicians, managers, etc. – in contrast to citizens and patients. Harrison *et al.* (1992) offer a particular perspective on the process of 'agenda setting' whereby a dominant group may control agendas in such a way that it promotes and protects its general dominance. This does not necessarily involve conflict, and often happens without the powerful having to act, as their dominance appears implicit in the political process. Rapid Appraisal intends to open up the debate about power, its foundation and the ways in which interdependence can be established in order to create an equilibrium whereby the previously powerless are enabled to shape agendas in health.

Sharing power raises a number of problems, and within most developed countries these are framed by increasing resource constraints within the public sector. Several countries have formulated an overall strategic framework for making choices in health care and where communities have been involved in making those choices (e.g. Dunning, 1992). Research is beginning to emerge highlighting the difficulties in asking communities and individuals to exercise power and choice. One key dilemma is when communities' values are diametrically opposed to professional, managerial or political values. This dilemma goes beyond the scope of research methodology and enters the realm of ethics. However, Chapter 5 will argue that Rapid Appraisal cannot avoid this particular problem and will have to search for a solution of how to weigh up the community perspective against others. Furthermore, the interest of communities in influencing resource allocation more generally may be crucially important in terms of political acceptability and sustainability of public sector reforms (Saltman, 1992).

Chapter 6 examines key methodological issues by focusing on the data collection and analysis in Rapid Appraisal. Many authors who have carried out Rapid Appraisals in the developing world rely on a varied 'tool kit' using both quantitative and qualitative methods, and create a methodological 'jigsaw' which is eclectic and flexible. An important feature of Rapid Appraisal, namely triangulation, will be discussed. In this case this means two things: first, comparing the two different ways of knowing, i.e. qualitative knowledge uncovering people's motivations, beliefs and so on, and quantitative knowledge about the specific case; second, establishing validity through mapping the different ways of understanding a phenomenon, in particular, contrasting the community perspective with that of policy-makers. It is important here to recognize that knowing is contextual and socially constructed – which in turn influences the process of determining needs and making choices.

An important criticism of Rapid Appraisal has been highlighted in a number of studies, namely its emphasis on change rather than continuity. In many of the developing country examples this is effected in an indirect manner through providing decision-makers with alternative knowledge derived from appraising the perspectives of those groups of people normally not heard. Whilst this is an essential contribution to the decision-making process, Rapid Appraisals in the developed world have attempted to go further and centrally involve the decision-makers themselves in uncovering these alternative perspectives. Thus, in theory, they are committed and accountable to the communities they have listened to. Following on from this, Chapter 7 will explore two issues: first, how change is defined, that is, whether clarity of purpose and the nature of change can be arrived at through a dialogue between policy-makers and communities; second, whether and how change can be sustained. Often, communities find a longer-term commitment equally important as change. This relates directly to the question of empowerment whereby communities are supported in ensuring that change can be embedded at both grass roots and institutional levels. The latter should lead to incorporating community knowledge in the policy process, while at the same time preserving its potential to challenge.

The future of Rapid Appraisal will be discussed in Chapter 8 where a summary will be provided of the strengths and weaknesses of the approach. Some have already been documented by authors working in the developing world (Kumar, 1994) while other issues have surfaced in applications in the developed world. For example, the emergence of new 'experts' in the community can lead to a misguided understanding of community needs. Primarily, this chapter will focus on the potential methodological development of Rapid Appraisal and its linkages with theoretical and strategic departures. One strand that will be discussed is the connection with futures research, where the centrality of visions and alternative scenarios is emphasized (Bezold, 1994). Rapid Appraisal's strength is in allowing the community to set priorities that inform policy. This is an ideal foundation for developing a vision with communities which can guide strategy and policy of a number of agencies working collaboratively. It can then lead to setting out a range of possible scenarios in order to clarify priorities which form a cumulative programme for shaping a desired future. At this point, top-down and bottom-up policy formulation converges and

Rapid Appraisal moves from being an agent for change to a catalyst for strategic visions.

The above outline of the key themes and how they are organized within the chapters of this book intends to clarify Rapid Appraisal as a method, and as an approach which conceptualizes a number of policy issues by connecting with contemporary theoretical debates. It may appear that Rapid Appraisal is discussed in a highly academic fashion. To some extent this is inevitable if the linkages are to be made with broader concepts. At the same time, this book also intends to offer practical ideas about how to plan and carry out a Rapid Appraisal. Most chapters are, therefore, organized into two sections. The first, and most detailed part, is the theoretical discussion; the second part offers a specific outline of 'how-to-do-it' and case examples relevant to the topic under discussion. For example, in Chapter 3 the concept of the community will be practically illustrated by offering various pragmatic solutions to the definition of a community, and examples of how this has been done in different settings. These practical hints will be boxed within each chapter and thus serve as an easy reference point. A final chapter draws all the practical points together and summarizes the development of Rapid Appraisal method in chronological order. It is hoped that the combination of a theoretical and practical approach will offer sufficient insight into the relevance and applicability of the Rapid Appraisal to policy-makers, service planners and academics in developed countries.

Setting up a Rapid Appraisal

A Rapid Appraisal can be used for two purposes, which could be separate or combined: first, Rapid Appraisal can be used as a diagnostic tool, that is to examine, describe and analyse particular community concerns. Often it is part of a larger programme of study which can encompass population health surveys, analysis of census and demographic data, focus group interviews and so on. Second, it can be used as an agent for change, where the community concerns are taken as point of departure for the development of an action programme focusing on improving the quality of life of the community or sections of that community. It can be argued that the most successful Rapid Appraisal combines both these purposes where it fits into a larger research programme which allows for more complex and in-depth understanding of community concerns, feeding into policies for change which are built upon an alliance of communities and decision-makers. In short, it is important to outline at the beginning the objectives of a Rapid Appraisal exercise, and the context within which it takes place.

The steps within a Rapid Appraisal can be broadly defined, but have to be understood in a flexible manner, as local circumstances can dictate alterations to the sequence. In later chapters we will discuss variations on the different steps, a range of innovations and possible further avenues to explore. At this stage an outline pattern can be offered (Table 1.1).

Table 1.1 Outline steps in Rapid Appraisal

Step 1	Defining purpose, target community and agencies involved.
Step 2	Project leader or team to prepare RA.
Step 3	Workshop with multi-agency, multi-disciplinary team.
Step 4	Fieldwork: observation, secondary data collection, interviews.
Step 5	Collation and analysis of data – formulation of needs list.
Step 6	Prioritization of needs.
Step 7	Feedback to community, discussion of action.
Step 8	Programme of change.
Step 9	Evaluation and redefinition of priorities.
Step 10	Second RA? Visioning of the future?

<table><tr><td>**2**</td><td># Conceptualizing health need</td></tr></table>

The ideas underlying Rapid Appraisal have various theoretical roots which make the method an approach both to conceptualizing health policy, and to understand needs. The philosophical link between the World Health Organization's definition of health as 'a state of complete physical, mental and social well-being and not merely the absence of disease or infirmity' (WHO, 1981) and Rapid Appraisal's focus on health rather than health care will form the starting point for the discussion. In approaching the issue of health from the perspective of assessing 'the extent to which an individual or group is able, on the one hand, to realize aspirations and satisfy needs and on the other hand to change or cope with the environment' (WHO, 1985), the analysis of need becomes central in this chapter. Furthermore, the purpose of Rapid Appraisal is to understand the needs of particular groups or communities, and thus an in-depth treatment of the concept of need, and health need, is essential if we are to explore the theoretical background to Rapid Appraisal.

An extensive body of literature developed by philosophers and economists, in particular, has furthered our understanding of need to a considerable degree. The intention here is to rehearse some of the essential arguments from recent research, and to apply them to the particular method and the contexts within which Rapid Appraisal is used. Therefore, this chapter will be limited to the discussion of need as universal or relative, and the way in which needs are expressed in different cultural forms. The possible convergence of different perspectives on need will be examined, and the limitations of established methods such as epidemiology will be touched upon. This will lead to an exploration of new territories such as the methodological development where the multiplicity of need perspectives can be brought together into a complex understanding of need and health need. Against this background Rapid Appraisal can be assessed in terms of its capacity to broaden and deepen the concept of need and its operation.

THEORIES OF HEALTH

The WHO definition of health marked a watershed in the concept of health in that it delineated a clear shift away from the medically dominated idea of health as an absence of disease, towards a holistic understanding of health which placed the individual within a social, economic and cultural context. Whilst being recognized as an important stimulus to the development of a 'new public health' reasserting the link between medicine and society (Ashton and Seymour, 1988) it also poses problems as to its conceptual clarity (what is complete health?) and its operational usefulness (does anyone enjoy complete health? how can it be measured?) (Abel-Smith, 1994). Furthermore, questions have been raised in relation to perspective, as the definition of health can vary between the expert definition of health and the subjective definition of those experiencing a state of health. It can be argued that the WHO definition is intended as a visionary definition, and thus should be used as a statement of intent. Yet, this does not resolve the problem of how the ideal state of health can be judged to have been achieved. How universal is the concept of health in this definition? Anthropologists, in particular, have argued that health is perceived differently in different cultures and general rules about health cannot easily be formulated (Worsley, 1982).

Focusing first on the WHO definition and its intentions, it has been argued that its main purpose is to supplant the medical definition of health with one that is based on an understanding of the causes of ill-health, namely as rooted in inequalities. The focus shifts towards a commitment to greater justice and equity in the allocation of resources, including health resources. Macdonald (1994) stresses that two other principles are equally important, that of participation and collaboration. Taken together, the WHO approach poses a major challenge to the medical model, and places health at the heart of the political process. This definition is attractive within the context of social justice, but this does not fully resolve the difficulties at the level of precision and clarity, nor at the level of implementation.

To take the latter first, Van der Geest and colleagues (1990) highlight that the strategy formulated by the WHO arising from their concept of health, the Primary Health Care (PHC) approach, poses similar conceptual confusions. They argue that PHC is a global movement, rather than a concrete strategy, and as a result it has multiple interpretations – some close to the original intentions, others perversely fashioned to maintain the status quo of inequality. In drawing together theoretical and empirical material they point out that the concept of health, and its strategic form of PHC, displays contradictions: it attempts to move away from medical rationality, while at the same time one of the principal objectives is to reduce mortality and morbidity rates – measured in epidemio-logical terms; community participation is envisaged as self-reliance and equal-ity, which are Western interpretations, and does not take into account the various cultural forms community participation takes. Van der Geest and colleagues (1990) quote the Nepalese interpretation of community participation as obeying orders from above to contribute land, money or labour to a specific development project (p.1027). They go on to analyse the contradictions which emanate from the imprecise definition of health and PHC, and document confu-sions at the level of governments, institutions, health workers and local commu-nities. This leads to the conclusion that PHC has no fixed meaning, but that it cannot be separated from its political context.

Taking up the issue of meaning, this can be analysed from a philosophical and a cultural perspective. Philosophers have long concerned themselves with the notion of health, on the one hand, because it is considered as a fundamental question about human well-being; on the other hand, because it directly relates to the provision of health care. The WHO definition of health is considered as too wide and utopian: no-one has ever had 'complete physical, mental and social well-being', so it cannot be preserved or restored by health workers (Garrard, 1994). A narrower definition, allowing the formulation of criteria for health, has been the aim for many philosophers, and attempts have been made to arrive at objective, value-free definitions. It is beyond the scope of this chapter (and the author's competence) to review the philosophical literature, but it is important partially to rehearse the line of argument in relation to health.

In a philosophical sense, objectivity allows definitions to be independent of individual or group opinion, and this can be carried through in attempts to define health. Like theoreticians from other disciplines, philosophers have often approached the question of health in opposition to disease and illness (Gillon, 1986), or developed wider notions such as 'malady' to encompass evil, such as death, pain, disability, loss of freedom or opportunity, or loss of pleasure (Culver and Gert, 1982, p.81). Hare (1986) takes a similar starting point and states that disease is a condition that generally is bad for organisms to have. 'Bad' is a normative term, implying that it has qualities which, other things being equal, *ought* to be avoided or remedied. The corollary is that disease should be avoided, and this has great practical (and policy) consequences in terms of the type, quantity and distribution of health care. The introduction of the notion of badness, however, requires some sort of evaluation, and it impor-tant to consider who evaluates: the doctors, the State, the sufferer and so on. Hare raises this as a crucial element in the discussion, but does not provide many indications of how to resolve contrasting or incomplete evaluations. Turning to the literature which examines the social construction of health, disease and illness can perhaps throw light on to this conundrum.

Cultural anthropologists emphasize the centrality of the body in understanding health: the physical body is a significant framework through which the moral order is represented (Richman, 1987). Thus, the meanings attached to the experiences of the physical body are social categories which sustain a particular view of society. In Western societies the body has been viewed as a biological organism, and distinctions can be drawn between disease as an abnormality in the structure or functioning of the body, which is largely determined by the prevailing ideas, values and meanings within a particular culture; illness as the (individual's) experience of disease as moulded by socio-cultural perceptions; and sickness as the societal validation of disease or illness (requiring the sick to play a particular social role, e.g. absolving them from certain social obligations) (Eisenberg, 1977). In reality, the dominant Western perspective has been disease-oriented and health services have largely been shaped by biomedical thinking. The anthropological insistence on the holistic and pluralist nature of health, tracing through the varied cultural experiences of individuals and groups, has called this medical domination into question. In this way attention is redirected to the importance of socio-cultural contexts in understanding behaviour, and health and being healthy are problematic concepts which cannot just be treated as the obverse of illness or disease (RUHBC, 1989).

Locating health within a socio-cultural context means that it cannot be understood without understanding the key concepts and values used within that context and how they fit together into a universal framework, which possesses its own conceptual and practical logic. Or to put it more strongly, health knowledge and behaviour form part of basic social institutions, and directly relate to contested arenas such as responsibilities, rights, power and authority (Bibeau, 1988). Whilst the connection between beliefs, behaviours and institutional requirements is important, this can simultaneously lead to an exaggerated cultural relativism whereby health cannot be defined at all. This criticism is disputed by Nicolson and McLaughlin (1987) who argue that a social constructionist approach to health and medicine allows intellectual and polemic questioning. For example, they state that sufferers might think about what shapes their own beliefs about health and illness, or medical professionals can reflect on their own practice, and realize the limited and fallible nature of medical knowledge. Thus, the way in which health is defined can be evaluated as to whether it is a product of a particular time and space, or whether it attempts to transcend a specific cultural context. In either case, a definition of health will result from this endeavour. The significance of the anthropological contribution lies in making explicit *who* evaluates health – precisely the issue that Hare (see p.12) touched upon. Health as a cultural concept makes the connection between what is considered to constitute health, and from whose perspective this is defined. Thus, health cannot be defined absolutely and precisely, but a social construction framework does allow clarity about the way in which health emerges as an evaluative concept, and therefore, its validity can be accepted or questioned on explicit grounds.

The above discussion has not resolved the vexed question of what health is, but attempted to demonstrate the puzzles surrounding the concept, and the ways in which various disciplines have addressed it. The WHO definition is obviously not without its problems, both in terms of the conceptual foundation and the implementation in policy and strategy. If, however, the definition is seen more as a statement of intent, rather than a precise delineation of the notion of health itself, it does provide a direction, namely shifting the focus towards equity and considering health within a broader social, economic and ecological context.

THEORIES OF NEED

Rapid Appraisal attempts to grasp the nettle of how to understand need from the vantage points of the multiplicity of perspectives, building upon the moral imperative to give voice to the needs of people who have limited access to power, and upon the reality of social and health policy which has to prioritize needs. The underlying approach is based upon implicit definitions of need, which have to be brought to the surface in order to appreciate the implications of aspiring to deliver a clear needs agenda. This must be based on priorities agreed between those who make and implement policy, and those who are the subject of policy. In order to analyse the concept of need within Rapid Appraisal we will draw on a number of authors who have explored the territory in relation to health and social policy.

One of the most widely quoted sources is Bradshaw (1972) who developed a taxonomy of social need, which in his own recent assessment (Bradshaw, 1994) was developed in a less harsh world and was never intended to have a practical intent. His distinction between four different types of need (normative, felt, expressed and comparative) has, however, been used extensively within the health and social field in order to define the various aspects of need, and raised awareness about the complexity of the term and the way in which it informs policy decisions. Bradshaw revisits his taxonomy and assesses the contribution of philosophers and economists before concluding that perhaps the notion of need is less useful as a target for health and social policy than the concept of inequality. Before jumping to the same, or a different, conclusion it is necessary to discuss a number of seminal contributions, and consider their impact upon the use of the concept of need within the Rapid Appraisal approach.

A major dilemma for policy-makers is that the concept of need is used in everyday language and decision-making, but the boundaries of the concept are unclear. The strict theoretical attempts at defining need have so far not proven useful in aiding the decision-making process. Doyal and Gough (1991) explicitly address the difficult problem of defining basic needs, and the relevance of this endeavour for policy-making. Their project is an ambitious one and they contend that 'objective and universal human needs can be identified both in theory and practice, and can be employed to assess the success of political and economic formations throughout the world' (Doyal, 1993, p.114). They argue that survival, physical health and autonomy are universal, basic needs: without physical survival individuals cannot act and reduced physical health disables social participation; in order to participate in any form of life individuals must have the ability to plan their life. Hewitt (1993) interprets these two basic needs as defining the essentially materialistic nature of human existence, and denoting the fundamental conditions for rational and self-determining human conduct when confronted with technical, moral and political choices.

For policy-makers the key question is whether a definition of universal, basic need becomes so abstract as to lose its usefulness; conversely, an empirical, politically relevant definition of need poses the danger of presenting so-called objective needs while obscuring their cultural relativity. Soper (1993) offers a wide-ranging critique of the Doyal and Gough argument and poses a number of questions which are relevant to our concerns. First, she argues that the intense focus on defining basic needs overlooks the significance of the form taken by the specific satisfiers of these needs. She points out that a causal relationship between the forms in which some are meeting basic needs and the forms in which others are being deprived can be pointed out. To be more specific, in providing government incentives for home ownership, resources are not made available for the extension of council housing. Thus, while an intermediate need such as shelter has been fulfilled in the achievement of the basic need for health, it has not been achieved equitably. A number of other questions are intimately bound up in this, such as the distinction between needs – which are fundamental to human well-being, and wants – conditions of further flourishing, or in the specific example, the distinction between the need for shelter and wanting to own a house.

Second, Soper draws a distinction between 'thin' theory, which attempts to determine universal need independent of cultural and subjective content, and 'thick' theory which looks at the experience of need within a given culture. The latter approach takes a democratic and participative stance, and can explicitly be on the side of the oppressed. However, this position cannot automatically be put into operation within Rapid Appraisal, as Soper warns of the danger that no satisfactory discrimination between needs and subjective preferences is made. In a policy framework this degree of subjectivity does not assist in making choices, and whilst Rapid Appraisal is a methodology aimed at allowing the voice of underprivileged groups to be heard, a touchstone for determining need is necessary.

On the other hand, overly emphasizing the objective and universal basis of need can lead to paternalism and dominance of expert definitions of need. Hewitt (1993) addresses this question explicitly and argues that it is consistent to uphold the view that certain needs have a real and objective status but which nonetheless appear in culturally different forms. He cites the work of Townsend (1979) as an example of overcoming the duality of objectivity and subjectivity in need. Townsend developed the concept of poverty based on an empirical and objective standard, and derived from that theory clear indicators of need (deprivation). The interesting issue put forward by Hewitt is how the objective perspective and the post-modern relativist position relate to each other, and he provides evidence from Desai's (1986) research of convergence between the socially relative and objective definitions of need. While this finding should not become a generalization, as we will see from the examples within Rapid Appraisal and other studies, it raises an important point as to when and on what issues does convergence take place, and whether this provides evidence for a more objective (or perhaps better termed inter-subjective) definition of need.

The third problem raised by Soper relates to the use of the objective approach within social and health policy. If we are to accept that needs are universal and basic, the discovery of needs is finite, that is, certain needs are defined as such, others are defined as wants or preferences. In particular, when applied to the present and the future, needs fulfilment is framed by considerations of limited resources that are available to meet welfare demands. In contrast, when the concept of relative need is applied, post-modern approaches argue that individuals and communities are free to define their own reality, and consequently all their needs are perceived necessities. This implies that the list of needs is potentially endless, and in policy terms one is confronted with the insoluble question of matching limited resources with needs that are all equally justifiable. While the democratic nature of this approach has to be recognized, in reality this is an untenable position on philosophical and historical grounds, that is, not all needs are equal, and there is a moral responsibility towards future generations not to exhaust resources so that they will have an equal chance to needs fulfilment.

This brings us to the last point, namely Soper's concern that physical health and autonomy cannot be seen as equally needed (or as Soper states, whether they are equally essential to the avoidance of serious harm). Although both are accepted as basic needs, the cultural context can place emphasis on one or the other need. This is important in Rapid Appraisal where it is possible that communities' concern with health, such as a safe environment, is less than their concern for autonomy, such as the need for emancipation of underprivileged groups. Perhaps this question of balance is less important than the recognition that while attempting to develop a universalist approach to need which provides an empirical and moral yardstick (Doyal, 1993), the rich tapestry of people's realities can still be acknowledged. Or as Soper(1993) puts it (this enterprise) 'may be an essential first move towards the implementation of those global welfare programmes of most practical import to the preservation of life, and promotion of cultural diversity, among the most deprived' (p.115).

Returning to Bradshaw, the above discussion about the concept of need, and the importance of understanding needs objectively within social and health policy, requires further elaboration. He (Bradshaw, 1994) argues that while we can accept the ideas behind the universalist approach, this does not necessarily help in addressing the policy questions as to the level of health or human development we are aiming at. He also refers to the economic paradigm which focuses on choice rather than need, and thus becomes more instrumental. This is echoed in the language used by many governments when discussing need. For example, the Dutch policy document on health care options for the future is aptly named 'Choices in health care' (Dunning, 1992) and explicitly places three perspectives alongside each other: the individual, medical-professional and community-oriented perspective. It is argued that the community perspective is most important, and this is determined by social values and norms. Three normative points are stressed which form the foundation of the approach, namely:

1. the fundamental equality of people as established in the constitution;
2. the fundamental need for protection of human life, as endorsed in the international conventions ratified by our country;
3. the principle of solidarity, as expressed in the organization and financing of the health care system (p.54).

It is the last point that emphasizes the centrality of choice, namely, that need is not equally distributed in society, and that certain needs will have priority over others. This is expressed in solidarity, whereby the healthy are in solidarity with the sick, and the wealthy with the poor. The commitment to addressing inequality in health is integral to this approach. A corollary is a concern with effectiveness and cost-effectiveness because the awareness of meeting a multitude of needs within a limited resource envelope shapes the nature and degree of solidarity.

In analysing the British approach to need, Bradshaw (1994) states that on the one hand there has been a growing obsession with the concept, while on the other hand government has been uncomfortable with the implications of using need as a basis for policy-making. The 1980s have actually seen the considerable narrowing of what is considered as need: for example, health need was defined in medical terms as 'the known ability to benefit from health care' (NHS Management Executive, 1990). Bradshaw quotes a number of other examples in the field of social policy, and concludes that the concept of need has increasingly been used cynically in order to 'camouflage policies which in their intention and effect have the explicit purpose of increasing inequalities' (p.49). This conclusion brings him closer to the Dutch approach by shifting the attention from a concern with defining need to understanding inequality.

The research on inequalities in health is extensive (for example, Townsend and Davidson, 1982; Illsley and LeGrand, 1987; Whitehead, 1992) but has never become central to British policy-making. Sir Douglas Black (1993) assessed the impact of this work and concluded that a wider strategy of social measures aimed at attacking inequalities has never been attempted, and that the reforms of health care are actually moving further away from such a goal. Bradshaw draws on this body of work when developing his argument that the association between inequalities and health remains very strong, or more precisely, that the distribution of income, the degree of inequality and the level of solidarity of a nation determines the levels of health. The wider focus on the distributive question of inequality is, according to Bradshaw, more fruitful than a narrower focus on needs and priorities which are circumscribed by the demands of a quasi-market in health care.

Yet, the concept of inequality is no less problematic than the concept of need. The evidence from the studies cited above centres around the association between deprivation and mortality (rather than morbidity). This association can be demonstrated at the level of general populations, and can be disaggregated to ward level. However, Sloggett and Joshi (1994) make an important observation when they state that 'the association is, in most cases, completely outweighed by personal factors' (p.1473). They illustrate this point by analysing data on 300 000 people from the longitudinal study of the Office of Population Censuses and Surveys. Their research highlights the complexity of using deprivation indices as a proxy for measuring inequality and targeting health and social policy. They draw attention to the interaction between area and personal circumstances, namely deprivation is a good indicator where the area indices overlap with a high concentration of personal disadvantage. For example, for men the increased risk of death associated with living in a deprived area was entirely explained by the levels of personal disadvantage experienced by the individuals. Conversely, if a disadvantaged individual lived in an area of relative affluence no protection from risk was received. Sloggett and Joshi conclude that health policy needs to target people as well as places.

The discussion around inequality has still to be sharpened up for it to provide guidance for policy. The framework outlined in the Dunning report will assist in focusing the issue by linking solidarity with inequality, while a comparison of the evidence from 'classics' such as Townsend with contemporary studies such as Sloggett and Joshi helps to provide a more objective basis to the relational aspects of inequality. While inequality is inherently a relational concept, and as such contains a subjective assessment of inequality of individuals or groups when compared against others, agreement has to be reached on when difference is defined as inequality. Townsend would argue that his approach defines a style of living. This can be measured, using both his approach or the combined focus on place and individual as advocated by Sloggett and Joshi. However, in policy terms the Dunning approach is necessary, which proposes that society has to reach consensus as to what constitutes serious impairment to social participation – thus judging the relevance of the objective measures. This has to take place at the national, macro-level of policy in order to avoid micro-level subjectivity which then paralyses decision-making. This is highly relevant for Rapid Appraisal which attempts to gauge the perspectives on need from policy-makers, professionals and communities, in order to arrive at a framework for defining priorities. Even though Rapid Appraisal takes place at the micro level, the broader questions about need and inequality are crucial if Rapid Appraisal is to question the basis of policy-making and its implementation.

Conceptual clarity about both need and inequality are important within Rapid Appraisal because the danger exists that cultural relativity dominates within the process and outcome. By attempting to access the disadvantaged and disempowered groups within society, and asking them to participate in the policy process, it is tempting to accept their definition of need as an objective reality, obscuring its cultural subjectivity. If Rapid Appraisal is to be useful as a policy tool, it must be capable of distinguishing need from want, difference from inequality; it is essential, therefore, to harness the rich tapestry of human experience within an objective and scientific framework for understanding need.

TOWARDS A METHODOLOGY FOR UNDERSTANDING NEED

Before attempting to formulate a methodological approach to assess needs – or inequality – and the forms in which needs can be met, it is necessary to discuss approaches which have traditionally been used to inform health policy. In most Western countries epidemiology has been the key methodology to provide the basis for determining need in populations, and which has set the parameters for resource decisions. Epidemiology has been defined, among other definitions, as 'the study of the distribution and determinants of health-related states or events in specified populations, and the application of this study to control of health problems' (Last, 1988). A number of recent publications have critically assessed the contributions and limitations of epidemiology in understanding health and health need, and the main arguments will be summarized here. In analysing the historical development of public health, and epidemiology as its core discipline, authors (RUHBC, 1989) detect a 'medicalization' of public health away from its community approach in order to achieve scientific status. Much emphasis has been placed upon the causal model when studying the determinants of health, but whilst causality is a problematic concept in dealing with organisms, it poses even greater difficulties when studying human behaviour.

For example, the link between smoking and lung cancer can be established, but exercising 'control' over the health problem requires a complex understanding of individual behaviour, social circumstances, cultural beliefs and so on.

Williams and Popay (1994b) provide an insightful analysis of the limits to epidemiology when focusing on health rather than disease. They elaborate on the point raised above and argue that the interplay between variables takes place at different levels and that the web of linkages made often do not provide clear causal explanations, but rather leave variance between groups or individuals uncertain. They raise two further points: first, studying the distribution of health problems requires the determination of 'cases'. This is again a terrain full of indeterminacy, and they offer the case of HIV/AIDS as an example. A number of people will not know whether they are HIV positive; another proportion will have reason to feel suspicious of official studies. Thus, the number of cases cannot necessarily be ascertained in a simple quantitative fashion. Second, epidemiology is less geared towards addressing the question of morbidity than mortality. For people suffering from a particular disease, the most important issues are the way in which their life is adversely affected. Thus, Williams and Popay argue, the question of prevalence is far from a straightforward determination of symptoms of disease, but one has to focus on the impact of disease on everyday life if health and health need are to be understood more clearly. The issues raised in this critique call into question the medico-scientific approach in epidemiology, and require methodological openness in order to capture the fullness of the human experience of illness.

Taking this a step further, and referring back to the argument by Bradshaw (1994) that inequality rather than health need, should be the guide for policy-making, the work by Vågerö (1995) is interesting. He makes the distinction between the public health significance of inequalities and the moral or theoretical importance attributed to these differences. The public health angle can be framed by the purpose of public health to improve the population's health in general, which means that not all difference is of equal importance, but depends on size, type of problem, and the potential improvements that can be made in dealing with a specific problem to the benefit of the population at large. The moral imperative lies in the equal right to health, which has to be considered regardless of size and contribution to general health. Cross-cutting these two elements is whether knowledge exists as to the factors which generate the difference (or inequality) and the plausibility of policies to influence this. Drawing these three strands together Vågerö states that the discussion about inequality has to include the public health significance, the causal factors (which most probably include Williams and Popay's broader interpretation) and the plausibility of change.

Alderslade and Hunter (1994) also concern themselves with the wider agenda for public health, and address the question of how public health should influence policy and practice. They revisit the core objective of public health as health improvement, and which connects knowledge and action. In order to realize the idea of public health management in action, health needs assessment is the starting point. In the same way as the authors discussed previously, they define needs not simply as 'epidemiological variables, but (as) complex social constructs which must be analysed, interpreted and given meaning and priority in conversation with the population served' (p.22).

The conclusion emerging from this discussion is that a new methodology for the assessment of needs is required given the limitations of the core discipline, epidemiology, in capturing the full meaning of the experience of ill-health. A methodology that can bring together the expert view (based upon medico-scientific premises) and the subjects' view (which focuses on the consequences of disease of everyday life) is now needed. Williams and Popay have started to address a number of the methodological issues and we will build on that work in order to formulate an approach which can bring together studies of universal needs, and studies of social and cultural perceptions of need. This enterprise is at the heart of Rapid Appraisal in its search for a consensus on needs so that policy can be formulated and owned by a wide constituency of stakeholders.

So, where do we go from here? The answer to this question is rather difficult in that needs assessment takes place within the real world where policy is made under conditions of political, financial and knowledge constraints. As a result needs assessment methodologies cannot be divorced from considerations about effectiveness and cost-effectiveness, priority-setting and the uneasy balance between individual or population health gain. One way forward has been proposed by Stevens and Raftery (1994) in their introduction to the wide-ranging epidemiological needs assessment reviews. They argue that there has been a change over time as to how need has been perceived, but that within the current British context – and in many other developed countries also – the central question does not revolve as much around who is needy (i.e. the need for health), but who needs what services (i.e. the need for health care). Following on from this argument, they define need in health care as the 'population's ability to benefit from health care' (p.12). They define health care broadly, including clinical care and preventive and supportive services; they also discuss the fluid boundaries around the concept of benefit which depend on the state of knowledge and cultural practices. Yet, their definition of need does not encompass the important reservations voiced by Vågerö, Williams and Popay and others, as the underlying assumptions are grounded in the disease based model which leaves little room for expansion towards a health improvement model, and the insertion of subjective experiences of illness. On the other hand, they seriously grapple with the interrelationships between needs (incidence and/or prevalence), effectiveness and cost-effectiveness and the pattern of existing services, in order to determine the direction of policy.

The building blocks for a new methodology for needs assessment have to come from diverse origins, which have already been outlined, but which will converge in the discussion that follows. The philosophical discussion of need emphasizes the importance of arriving at an objective (and universal) definition of need. When applying this principle to health policy-making, the example of the Netherlands made clear that real objectivity would be difficult to achieve, but that inter-subjectivity based on the widest possible inclusion of stakeholders (clinicians and other experts, policy-makers, the public, etc.) can lead to agreements about a needs profile at national and local levels. This broad consultation has to be underpinned by scientific evidence of the sort provided by Stevens and Raftery's reviews, which also assists in setting boundaries to the list of needs by determining cut-off points between needs and wants or preferences.

Soper (1993) places clarity of needs definition alongside the importance of recognizing cultural diversity, and anthropologists will take this stance further by arguing that needs cannot be understood outside of a cultural and historical context. This means that needs can change, depending on the state of knowledge, cultural values and political structures of control. For example, the technological advances in near patient testing, coupled with the spread of computers has meant that it is now possible for people to diagnose some of their own diseases at home (Economist, 1995). This can alter the patterns of need for prevention in certain population groups as they are controlling knowledge and elements of self-care. In turn, cultural perceptions of health and illness may shift. For example, the pressure from women's groups to de-medicalize childbirth in Western countries has transformed both the experience of childbirth to a more woman-centred one, and the nature of the services provided offering more choice to women. Needs in pregnancy and childbirth consequently are defined more holistically rather than pure clinically, and psychological preparation and social support are considered key needs.

The question of inequality in health continues to shape much of the debate around needs. The moral aspects of inequality (rather than difference) have a major impact of policy and again, a social consensus model will help to place the notion of inequality on a more objective footing. As a corollary, needs arising from inequality can be defined in terms of inhibitors to individuals and groups achieving their full potential to participate as members of society. Inequality as a relational concept is then integrated with the cultural frameworks dominant within a particular society, and the trap of excessive relativism can be avoided by making the criteria and parameters explicit. This can be done in the scientific manner as proposed by Townsend's deprivation index (1979), by consensus (Dunning, 1992) or formulating moral frameworks which link a person's equal right to health to fair equality of opportunity (Vågerö, 1995).

Creating a coherent needs assessment methodology built on the objective or inter-subjective definition of need, and taking into account cultural diversity and the centrality of inequalities, is a daunting task. The current state of knowledge remains incomplete and thus we are only partially prepared for this task. Rapid Appraisal has to be viewed within this developmental context, namely as contributing to the debate and to the methodological experimentation necessary for assessing needs in a rigorous and complex manner.

Needs assessment in Rapid Appraisal

A central purpose of Rapid Appraisal is to define a community's perspective on priority needs in order to influence local policy-making. The assessment of needs cannot be made by communities alone, if they are to make an impact on policy. Thus, an essential aspect of the needs assessment exercise is to integrate the expert view (predominantly the epidemiological and management/resource perspective), with the lay view which is embedded in the cultural experience of needs and health needs.

The origins of Rapid Appraisals in health can be traced back to the WHO Health for All 2000 strategy, and consequently the definition of health used relies heavily on the WHO definition (Annett and Rifkin, 1988). We have argued previously that this definition has to be considered as a statement of intent rather than a strict definition which can be operationalized, and we will apply that idea here.

The point of departure is that health needs have to be viewed as part of more general needs, which means that the holistic concept of health underlies Rapid Appraisal. First, the role of science in needs appraisal lies in the collation and assessment of existing epidemiological material about a particular community. This includes the patterns of disease and disability, and the use of resources within a community. The latter is reflected in activity data from health and social services compared to available information about effectiveness and cost-effectiveness. Second, cultural perceptions of need are gathered through interviews with individuals and groups exploring their interpretations of need in order to understand the narrative logic of their experiences, and the context within which they make sense. Third, by bringing the different perspectives together a (moral) framework can be constructed which defines the parameters of need based on inter-subjective consensus.

The methodological choices concerning the gathering of data will be discussed in Chapter 6, and the way in which consensus can be achieved about priorities will be discussed in Chapter 5. The purpose of this chapter is to create an integrated approach to the different interpretations of need, and Annett and Rifkin (1988) have designed an information profile which connects the different levels and categories which feed into an understanding of need.

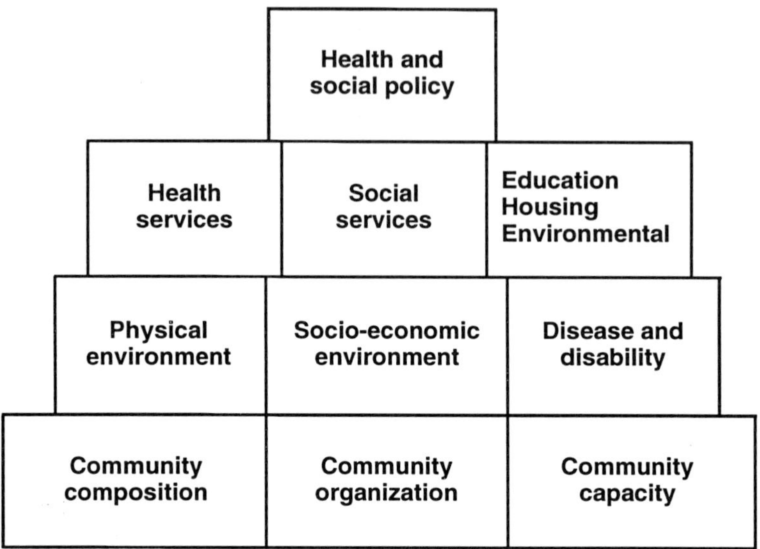

Figure 2.1 Information profile. (Adapted from Annett and Rifkin, 1988.)

In a Rapid Appraisal information must be collected on each of the boxes of the information profile, which will then be integrated into a coherent whole. Taking each of the categories in turn the type of data required can be summed up as follows:

- Community composition: a description of the demographic characteristics of the population which are indicative of the way the community can operate as a community. For example, if a large section of the population is aged 75 and over, this has consequences for support systems, financial resources available, patterns of disease and disability and so on.
- Community organization and structure: a description of the way the community organizes its relationships serves as an indication of the nature and strengths of informal networks. For example, do self-help groups, mother and toddler groups, luncheon clubs exist? Do local councillors or MPs form a focal point for the community, or do churches play an important role?
- Community capacity: the capacity of a community to support the individuals and groups within depends on the two above-mentioned categories. An assessment of the inner resources of a community is required in order to estimate whether community initiatives can be sustained, and to ascertain the balance between the formal and informal sectors.
- Physical environment: a description of the physical environment forms the basis of an analysis of how this external environment impacts on the quality

of life of the inhabitants. For example, if the area is cut through by dangerous roads, or is under the smoke of an industrial estate there will be implications for health and safety which have to be understood both in quantitative and qualitative terms.

- Socio-economic environment: employment and education opportunities are important elements determining the well-being of individuals and communities. Thus, an audit of those opportunities and a community view of their appropriateness, acceptability and accessibility form an essential part of the information pyramid.
- Disease and disability: an epidemiological and experiential assessment of the pattern of disease and disability provides the basis for a health needs assessment of the community. For example, the number and degree of health problems can be ascertained through secondary data sources, and complemented by an understanding of the consequences of those health problems on people's participation and quality of life.
- Health services: a description of the type of services available will be sought, and an assessment of their appropriateness, acceptability and accessibility to the community. This also has to involve services at secondary and tertiary level, alongside the primary and community level.
- Social services: the same type of information as for health will be collated.
- Education, housing, environmental services: as above, but relating to these sectors.
- Health policy: the way in which health policy targets the community and develops specific strategies to address local problems will be examined. This can include both general and local policies, and an assessment has to be made as to whether the community is part of, or has an awareness of, those policies.

The various data sources for the construction of the information profile leads to a 'dense' picture of a community. Rather than writing an anthropological analysis of the way the community operates, the purpose of the Rapid Appraisal is to condense this information and extract a list of key concerns which can then be presented to the community. They then engage in a priority setting exercise which leads to a specific and targeted priority listing for action (see Chapter 7).

Examples

In the Sandown community high unemployment was the most commonly discussed feature. There were no hard figures, and estimates fluctuated from 30% to 70%, but the degree of poverty arising from unemployment was clearly noticeable. People were saying that they felt guilty about being in debt, and the attitude of professionals often exacerbated this. The impact on health was immediate and invariably detrimental, often resulting in feelings of apathy and hopelessness. The issues were reflected in a number of categories:

- Community organization: fear and apathy, lack of finance for leaders.
- Community capacity: sense of hopelessness, sense of decline, no experience of positive change, lack of self-respect.
- Socio-economic environment: unemployment, poverty, no prospects for young people.
- Disease and disability: poverty as health risk.

In Woodforde a number of health concerns were voiced, related partly to the physical environment, and partly to actual health service provision. First, in the area most of the streets were narrow, causing traffic congestion and hazards for pedestrians. Access for emergency services has been a problem. Second, people felt that local hospital facilities should be available, and emphasized this need for people with mental health problems in particular. Also, school medicals were considered an important protection against child abuse. The issues were highlighted as follows:

- Physical environment: traffic hazards due to narrow streets, no safe play areas for children.
- Health services: area needs its own hospital, long waits before hospital admission (especially for the elderly), concern that school medicals may be removed, people with mental health problems need more help, improved family planning service needed.

The descriptive accounts are important for contextualizing the specific issues that are deducted from them, but the focus of the Rapid Appraisal is on the key issues which can be described in short sentences. In terms of this chapter's discussion, these issues are considered to represent the community needs and will have to be validated in the next stage, when they are presented to the community for assessment. This will be compared with the assessment of experts (professionals and managers/resource holders) in order to arrive at an inter-subjective judgement of priorities. The process of prioritization will be made transparent through explaining the procedures used for priority-setting (weighting, computer-assisted calculations, etc.) which will be discussed in Chapter 5.

Community involvement in policy-making

 3

The launch of the WHO Health for All 2000 approach brought together much of the more progressive thinking about community involvement in health. Since then, there has been much debate, a multitude of experiments world-wide have been developed and an equal amount of lip service is being paid to the concept of community involvement. At the same time, there is considerable variation in interpretations of the concept, the way it should be implemented in policy and strategy, and assessment as to whether community involvement improves the quality of policy-making in health.

This chapter will draw on some of the impressive work that has been carried out in health, and other fields, using community involvement principles. It will also go back further and rehearse the sociological debates concerning the concept of community itself, and in particular, the distinction between the empirical description of what communities are, and the normative description of what community life should be (Newby, 1987). Certainly, in policy circles these two descriptions are often conflated, causing a lack of clarity of purpose in how decision-makers can relate to communities. We will attempt to formulate definition of community which assists decision-makers to understand the target of their policies, and therefore allows them to see better with whom they are trying to collaborate.

The second task is to examine the notion of involvement which has to be understood as a structural and political issue. The contradictions between health systems which are centralized, and geared towards compartmentalized, curative health care, and the democratic conditions which are required for genuine participation to take root and be maintained, will be explored. The related discussion of power is addressed in Chapter 4, but here we will look in particular at the way in which relationships between communities and policy-makers are shaped, both structurally and ideologically. In bringing together the discussions on community and involvement an assessment of the way in which these two concepts are used in Rapid Appraisal can take place. A number of examples serve as illustrations of community involvement in setting priorities in health, and various variations on this main approach will be discussed.

THE CONCEPT OF COMMUNITY

The analysis of Hillery (1955) is by now a well-known sociological tale: namely that as a result of his review of the literature which yielded 94 definitions of community, he concluded that the only common factor was that they all dealt with people. Notwithstanding this proliferation of research, and resulting definitions, it is important to provide a degree of conceptual clarity in order to arrive at a description of community that can work within a policy context. A number of authors have argued that the term community is too slippery, and has been misused in policy formulation in order to serve particular purposes. This is most notable in the policies of the conservative government in Britain which have promulgated the idea of the community as a populist concept, where a group of individuals work together in their own interest in opposition to the State. This approach goes hand-in-hand with the notion of the family which provides care and takes responsibility for the individuals within it, and the development of care in the community policies extends this ideal of self-reliance and informal care (Dalley, 1988). While the criticism of the current confused use of the term community is understandable, it is difficult to find an obvious replacement which provides a theoretical coat hanger for policy analysis, and the development of alternative policy. Therefore, it could be argued that unpacking the term remains important.

Both within the literature concerning community involvement in the developing world and the developed world, theoretical work has been carried out which attempts to elucidate the term community. It is beyond the scope of this chapter to review the full range, and many others have already done this most competently (for example, Oakley, 1989; Mayo, 1994). We will draw on some of the key contributions in order to clarify the theoretical underpinning of the use of the word community in Rapid Appraisal.

In tracing the historical roots of the term community Williams (1976) argues that in the 19th century the distinction between community, expressing more direct, more total and more significant relationships, and the State, representing the more formal, more abstract and more instrumental relationships, was drawn. He continues that this distinction has remained evident until this century, and in particular draws attention to the notion that community politics can be distinguished from national and local politics, in that it focuses on various kinds of direct action and local organization, emphasizing the 'working directly with people' (p.66). This latter insight is significant for the way in which Rapid Appraisal formulates its relationships with local communities. Another historical analysis has been carried out by Yeo and Yeo (1988) who categorize communities as a community of mutual caring, a community of service and the community as the State. The first category encompasses communities which are built around social relationships that are mutually supportive, the second category develops the idea of formal organizations providing services in a more philanthropic sense, while the third category allows the State to invoke particular ideals as in the interest of 'the community'.

The concern that Newby (1987) has expressed about the distinction between descriptive and normative definitions of community has exercised many sociologists. Because of what Williams (1976) called the tendency to use community as a 'warmly persuasive word' not all research has been able to disentangle the desirable (that is, the community as a network of supportive relationships) from the fact (a conglomerate of networks which can be equally supportive and destructive). It is, therefore, important to order the multitude of definitions into three broad types (Newby, 1987, pp.239–240):

- Community as locality: a human settlement located within a fixed and bounded local territory.
- Community as a set of social relationships which take place wholly, or mostly, within a locality.
- Community as a sense of shared identity.

While these three types are not mutually exclusive (Bulmer, 1987) it is important to make conceptual distinctions in order to understand the basis for defining a particular grouping as a community, and to clarify the way in which policy focuses on particular communities. Placing the analysis of communities within a wider context is necessary as the traditional and locally bounded networks are in decline as a result of many changes in the geographical, economic and political environment. In the developing and the developed world employment opportunities are not confined to localities, and the global market does not only create upheavals within nations from rural to urban centres, but across the world from less to more developed countries. The result is paradoxical: on the one hand, boundaries are shifting, and people's attachments are more widely spread, on the other hand relationships tend to be more privatized (Bulmer, 1987). The latter can perhaps be explained as seeking a degree of cohesion – kin, neighbours, friends – in an uncertain world.

Before we jump to the conclusion that the 'community-saved' theory (Mayo, 1994) is alive and well, one has to consider conflict and discontinuity within communities. Within the developing world divisions in communities have often been glossed over, and government agencies have worked with community leaders who pursued their own sectional interests or resisted attempts to share power (see example in Rifkin, 1990). Many policies on community care ignore inequalities within communities. In both the developing world, where programmes involve women in health and social care (Ong, 1986) and in the developed world, where women are implicitly expected to provide much of the informal care in the community (Parker, 1990, 1993), gender inequalities have been reinforced.

A second issue to consider is that communities are dynamic, and their definition of themselves changes as a result of wider social movements or specific events which influence communities' self-image. The impact of migrant labour in many developing countries has recreated community life in rural areas, where the male breadwinner is absent for long periods of time, and households are headed by women who have to take on tasks and responsibilities without the support of another adult, and often shoulder the heaviest burden of poverty (Sen and Grown, 1988). The impact of major events can also transform a community's image, and for example, the impact of HIV and AIDS has profoundly affected the way in which the gay community in many western countries perceives and organizes itself (Plummer, 1988). Given the potentially fluid nature of a community's identity policy-makers have to be clear when and how they identify communities and the way in which policies are geared towards the needs of those communities. Bulmer (1987) discusses that secondary structures have to be created which nurture attachments within communities, but the question of this creative process, the way in which objectives, leadership and membership have to be defined, have according to him been largely ignored. This opens up the debate as to how the voice of communities can actually be heard in policy-making.

Fundamental to the analysis is the way in which community life is understood. The political 'right' implicitly assumes that a caring community exists, which underpins the Victorian values of self-reliance and independence (Jack, 1983). Over the last decade the oppressive consequences of this philosophical starting point have become abundantly clear within the British context where an aggressive policy of care in the community has been pursued to the point of destruction (Wistow, 1995). In contrast, the analysis provided by Dalley (1988) of the concept of collectivism allows progressive ideas about community living to be explored. She discusses the theoretical variations of the concept, but we will concentrate on the second part of her argument, namely the practical components of collectivism, as they have most relevance for policy-making.

Collectivism can be understood under three broad headings (Dalley, 1988, pp.45–46): first, collectivism can be seen as social responsibility for all members of society. This can be held at the level of the State, but for our purpose the way in which it operates at the community level is most relevant. Responsibility can include a wide range of areas, such as welfare, resources and services for the community or specific groupings within. The well-being of the members of the community is central to this interpretation, which can be translated into particular objectives within a Rapid Appraisal. Second, collectivism is related to the domain in which it operates. This can be the public domain, such as for example health care and welfare systems, but it can also operate in the private domain, such as the informal sector of care. Exploitation of the latter domain has been exposed within feminist analysis, and Dalley argues that the breaking down of the public/private divide is central to the feminist enterprise. Third, there are numerous forms in which collectivist principles can be expressed, but one of the key contributions to the debate has again come from the feminist tradition, which proposes that consciousness about collectivism has to straddle the boundaries of the political and the personal. Concretely, this entails engaging in a debate on whether and how the organization of daily living reflects collectivist principles, and the way in which the domestic sphere can be transformed to become more collectivist. Dalley concludes that the term collectivism provides greater clarity than the term community; however, the continued widespread use of community in both the theoretical and policy literature makes it difficult to abandon the term altogether.

Drawing together these various strands of the debate, it is perhaps possible to build on the argument that Wellman (1979) has put forward, which takes into account the empirical reality that community cannot be strictly defined, yet contains certain core elements. The flexible approach that is proposed defines a community in terms of a locality and shared interests, but simultaneously focuses on the centrality of social networks and the ties of individuals and families. This appears to include the collectivist ideas of shared responsibility, the fluid boundaries between the public and private domains and the realization that communities are dynamic entities. This forces a move away from a unitary definition of communities which has led so many policies, towards a changing concept that is defined from the bottom-up, and demands that policy-makers listen to communities in order to gain insight into their self-perception, the way in which needs are defined and priorities are set. Such an approach requires a fundamental re-orientation of the way in which policy-makers work with communities, and automatically draws our attention to the question of involvement in policy formulation.

COMMUNITY CONSULTATION OR COMMUNITY INVOLVEMENT?

From the outset we have to be clear about the boundaries of this discussion as there is considerable confusion about the terminologies involved. First, we are not concerned here with consumers of health care or patients. While this is an important area of research and action, and a number of important lessons can be learned from comparative typologies (Saltman, 1992), and work on advocacy and brokerage for specific client groups (like people with physical handicaps or mental health problems) (NCVO, 1991; Wertheimer, 1991), this chapter addresses general populations. It focuses on the involvement of communities in the definitions of needs (including health needs), setting priorities and developing policy and strategy. As a result, the debate centres around the definition of involvement and its political and social context. It also connects directly with the above discussion of how decision-makers relate to communities and whether equity is included in the shaping of involvement.

Involvement is a difficult concept, both theoretically and pragmatically, and has been misused in so many ways as to be in danger of losing credibility. Yet, it offers genuine opportunities to alter fundamentally the way in which policies are designed and acted upon, and therefore, it remains important to clarify the use and abuse of the term. First, involvement and participation are often used interchangably denoting the same principles. Here, we will use the term involvement which Oakley (1989) endorses in his review of different approaches of community involvement in health which 'is a process by which partnership is established between the government and local communities in the planning, implementation and utilization of health activities in order to benefit from increased local self-reliance and social control over the infrastructure and technology of primary health care' (p.13). This definition seems appropriate in relation to Rapid Appraisal as it equally is concerned with a local emphasis and with health services within a primary health care context – taking into account the wider structure of other factors impinging on health.

A number of questions arise from the above discussion: first, a clear distance is taken from conflating involvement as a means or as an end. The former approach has the appearance of involvement, but in reality is asking people to participate in achieving pre-determined objectives. This has happened in many development projects where the resources of local people have been exploited and control over decision-making has not shifted to communities (Oakley, 1989). In developed countries this process has taken place in similar implicit ways, and Joule (1993) argues that involvement is often confused with consumer rights, which, though important are no substitute for community involvement in wider issues. Thus, the increased reliance on policy initiatives such as the 'Local Voices' approach (NHSME, 1992), which emphasizes that purchasers have to listen to local people when setting their strategies, have been criticized for obscuring the undemocratic nature of the British NHS.

Pollock (1992) and Pfeffer and Pollock (1993b) put forward the argument that there is an inherent tension with the idea of involving local communities within an internal market for health care. The objectives of involvement are concerned with choice, accountability and empowerment, while the internal market is concerned with efficiency and shaping choices. Furthermore, the health care market is increasingly being managed in contradictory ways (Paton, 1995), thus confusing the role of purchasers as assessors of needs and in building their relationship with local communities. The resulting polarization – to increase both central regulation and local planning – reinforces the argument from Pollock and Pfeffer, that the tension between a market logic and local accountability is irreconcilable. The conclusion that, in this instance, community involvement should be replaced by the term consumer consultation, making explicit that involvement is considered a means rather than an end, seems warranted.

In contrast, community involvement as an end places emphasis on the process of creating and/or reinforcing the confidence and solidarity among local people, and builds up influence and involvement in decision-making from the bottom-up (Oakley, 1989). In this participatory approach the recipient rather than the provider is central to the process (Hildebrandt, 1994) and thus negotiation, compromise, advocacy and so on are all key aspects of this process. One has to recognize that community involvement in the management, development and implementation of health care and other public systems is extremely complex, not least because it calls into question the distribution of power (Hawker, 1989). This issue will be addressed in the next chapter, but it must be noted that in many cases a naive approach to community involvement has been advocated which underplays the resistance to sharing or shifting power.

It is salutary to take cognisance of the historical review carried out by Croft and Beresford (1992) who have outlined the cyclical nature of the history of participation, and how little has been learned from past failures – or successes. This, they argue, has been largely because little systematic evaluation has been carried out on participation. On a more theoretical level, significant omissions in analysis can be detected, mainly the structural understanding of the role of the State and the market. The critique outlined in the previous paragraph is echoed by Croft and Beresford when they draw on Arnstein's (1969) ladder of citizen participation. They state that most initiatives remain on the two bottom rungs, namely therapy or manipulation, because of their failure to tackle the structural question. This, of course, is an extremely complex issue because it has to reconcile on one hand 'the need to resolve the tensions between universal principles and policies, and (...) the recognition of diversity, on the other' (Williams, A., 1992, p.10). Concretely, health and social policy have to be designed in such a way as to provide maximum protection to individual rights, and therefore, be concerned with questions of equity, access, cost-effectiveness and so on. At the same time, the different needs of individuals have to be recognized and space has to be created to allow these to be articulated. The opportunities for involvement which question the values underlying the dominant policy-making model, are slim indeed, and Croft and Beresford acknowledge that moving towards the creation of a participatory health or social policy model will not happen without struggle. The active involvement of local communities in this endeavour should not just be seen in a negative light, that is, wresting power from the hands of current decision-makers, it can also be considered as enabling the creation of a more responsive health policy which recognizes diversity, and therefore, can be better focused on equity and needs in order to make optimal use of scarce resources. This means that we have to examine more critically the way in which these notions can be put into practice.

MODELLING COMMUNITY INVOLVEMENT

These ideas are founded in the approach taken by the WHO, and accepted by many countries all over the world. Yet, the actual implementation of the principles of equity and participation is very variable, depending on the commitment of decision-makers. It is, therefore, important to be able to distinguish rhetoric from reality, and the model of participation, formulated by Rifkin, Muller and Bichmann (1988) assists in making this type of assessment. They engage in a similar discussion as advanced in this chapter about the concept of community, and add a definition that is important within a health context, namely the target or 'at risk' group. This definition is necessary for justifying differential resource allocation decisions within an equity framework.

Following this discussion they consider the term participation, and argue that three characteristics are essential: first, participation has to be active; second, it must involve choice; third, the choice must have the possibility to be effective. Rifkin and colleagues shift the emphasis from the impact of participation to its process, and set out a framework which describes the key factors influencing participation (p.933):

1. needs assessment;
2. leadership;
3. organization;
4. resource mobilization;
5. management;
6. focus on the poor.

The first five factors can be measured over time by marking a point on a continuum, ranging from wide participation (community people plan, control and use professionals as a resource) to narrow participation (where professionals maintain control over all processes with no community involvement). The measurement against these indicators allows comparisons in participation over time, between different assessors and between different participants. The five factors are placed together into a spoke configuration in order to illustrate the varied relationships between the factors. The sixth factor is crucially important as an indicator for equity, but cannot be measured on a continuum in the same manner as the other five, mainly because it operates on a much longer time frame.

This methodology is not evaluative in the sense of denoting whether community participation is good or bad. Neither is it intended to correlate directly community participation with improved health status. Finally, it indicates the level of direct participation, but cannot provide a similar descriptive analysis about social participation as this depends on the nature of social relationships and inequalities within a particular society, which requires an in-depth and longitudinal approach. Rather, the methodology is descriptive in terms of show-ing change in the short to medium term and the participatory processes associ-ated with this change. As such it allows a better understanding of the way in which broad participation builds on a range of activities and on the involvement of different sections of a community, and thus places health within a wider social context.

Whilst the above methodology is more descriptive than analytical, it provides a first step to actually providing both a baseline against which to assess changes in community participation, and to gain insight into the processes which move participation into the realm of empowerment and taking control. It could be argued that Rifkin and colleagues' emphasis on process has to be counterbal-anced by a more focused attention on the results of participation, because the way in which scarce resources are to be utilized is of central importance to communities. Only in seeing through the decision-making processes to an agreed outcome does community participation deliver its promise, and begin to create a basis for sustainability in shared policy-making.

A further step from the framework formulated by Rifkin and colleagues needs to incorporate the measurement of impact from the perspective of the various stakeholders. In this, the perspective of communities is central, but the evaluation of professionals and managers cannot be ignored: their knowledge, particularly in the area of epidemiology, can provide a comparative analysis, and place choices into a broader context. Or put in another way, the particulari-ties of a community's needs have to be weighed up against more universal needs. In order for the process and impact of community participation to be assessed in an integrated manner, a clear structure to community involvement has to be agreed between communities and policy-makers. This includes the definition of clear objectives, the way in which choices are to be made, and how the action plans resulting from those choices are to be translated into short- and medium-term strategies. The relationship between communities and policy-makers has to be negotiated and explicitly stated in terms of roles and responsi-bilities, and in particular, how the balance between change and continuity is to be achieved (see Chapter 7).

Elaborating on the approach outlined by Rifkin and colleagues, a more objec-tive assessment of impact has to be developed. Hawker (1989) offers a few pointers for this enterprise when outlining participatory processes with a posi-tive outcome. He utilizes the following indicators that could arguably be plotted on a similar continuum as Rifkin *et al.*'s indicators: people's own capacities and skills are developed; efficiency is improved as decision-makers learn from participative interaction. Hawker mentions a number of other indicators which cannot be equally clearly determined, such as, people feeling a sense of dignity and self-respect, the discovery of people's own real interests or the increase in mutual understanding between communities and policy-makers. As with focusing on the poor, these kinds of indicators represent ethical values and serve as an intent rather than an indicator. Yet, they provide an overall 'feel' for the direction and depth of change, and whether progress is made in terms of a shift in power.

The paradox existing at the heart of many contemporary health systems is that on the one hand resource-intensive care requires a rationalization of services, and more centralized decision-making; on the other hand, the increased emphasis on community involvement demands the existence of structures which allow local and democratic decision-making. Whether communities are defined as localities, as a network of shared interests, with or without collectivist tendencies, the tension between community participation and centralized policy-making continues to be problematic in terms of formulating a coherent philosophy for democratic involvement and its implementation. Perhaps the pragmatic approach, targeted at the organizations which are charged with making health policy provides the best chance of tackling this contradiction. Upton and Taylor (1995) argue that for the British health authorities, who are responsible for purchasing health care, and are supposed to be 'champions of the people', public (community) involvement can be developed successfully. Three conditions need to be fulfilled: first, senior managers must understand and have a practical commitment to public involvement. Specific senior people must be explicitly given responsibility to integrate the community perspective into strategic purchasing. Second, there has to be cadre within the organization with skills and confidence to engage in community involvement activity and to gain credibility with communities and other organizations. Third, a positive organizational culture which actually values community perspectives, and compares those with professional knowledge has to be created.

This approach can be considered top-down, but does not necessarily close off the bottom-up approaches which have been promulgated by most researchers and practitioners who draw on the WHO HFA2000 philosophy. The current reality in many countries is that the form of quasi-markets in health care disguises the nature of more centralist policy-making. The traditional dictum of grass roots policy-making falls short within the harsh practice of allocating scarce resources, and the idea of community participation has to operate in an almost opportunistic fashion, that is, to create openings in contradictory health policy-making and to utilize them in order to insert and strengthen community participation. Thus, the tendency to invoke public involvement as a means can be turned into it becoming an end by demonstrating that particular goals, such as health improvement, can be achieved more effectively and efficiently through involving communities in the assessment of need and making choices. The language of the market can be hijacked in order to engage a broad spectrum of perspectives from both communities and professionals in developing a needs-led strategy, which simultaneously serves the interests of communities. Rapid

Appraisal is a powerful tool for putting this into practice by creating a bridge between decision-makers and communities, and in particular through carefully researching community perceptions, relationships and interest groups.

In order to clarify the above theoretical issues we will now turn to the way in which Rapid Appraisal addresses the key questions of how to define communities, and how to harness participation.

Community definition in Rapid Appraisal

Rapid Appraisals in health have been carried out in developing and developed countries and have brought together the public, voluntary and private sectors with communities. The multi-disciplinary nature of Rapid Appraisal demands a broad participation from various organizations, but this has to be counterbalanced with a tight focus on a specific community in order to avoid the danger of becoming too wide-ranging and reconciling too many varied interests. Thus, the complexity of a multi-sectoral and multi-disciplinary approach is offset by focusing on small, defined communities. This means, in practice, that Rapid Appraisal looks at a size between 10 000 and 12 000 population which are concentrated in a particular locality. At the same time it takes cognisance of the other important variable, namely the shared interests, which can be preliminary gauged on the basis of socio-economic indicators or epidemiological stability (that is, similarity in morbidity and mortality patterns). If information is available, the choice of community can also be based on the way in which relationships and networks are structured. In general, Rapid Appraisals have taken place in localities which have little access to decision-making and policy formulation (often coinciding with socio-economic deprivation).

In most instances, policy-makers have felt the necessity, as part of their overall strategic role, to develop approaches involving communities. Often, they are not clear about the way in which community participation is to be defined, and certainly, are often not fully aware of the debates surrounding consultation versus participation and empowerment. This offers opportunities to promote the Rapid Appraisal methodology as it assists in community profiling, but also raises consciousness in decision-makers as to the real value of community perspectives for needs assessment, priority setting and using resources in a targeted and effective way. In the process, communities can gain knowledge and skills in working with policy-makers and their organizational structures. The objectives for genuine participation are easier to achieve when communities are relatively cohesive in terms of geography and common interests, because internal contradictions can be minimized in view of the collective perspective. This does not mean that divisions within communities should be glossed over, but assessed on their real impact and relevance for the majority of people. The criteria for determining the boundaries of a community have to be explicit so that no ambiguity exists about the inclusion (or exclusion) of particular groupings. This is extremely important for establishing legitimacy in setting objectives, determining strategy and actions which carry the approval of the majority of the community.

In practice, therefore, the decision of which community to involve in a Rapid Appraisal has to be based upon the maximum amount of information available, such as epidemiological data, census data, local health and social care profiles, information from voluntary organizations on specific interest groups and so on.

The other avenue into communities has been following a request from communities themselves, or people working with them, to carry out a Rapid Appraisal. For example, a Rapid Appraisal was carried out in a London borough at the request of a local General Practitioner who wanted to develop closer links with other agencies in order to address the holistic needs of the local population. He had the support from the community which considered itself as relatively neglected by policy-makers: it fell just outside the criteria used for inner-city deprived communities and thus attracted no extra support or funding. It was felt that a Rapid Appraisal could help in drawing attention to their needs, and attract more assistance from the statutory sector in particular.

Community participation in Rapid Appraisal

The discussion about the boundaries of communities has not addressed the issue of 'who is the community?'. In research terms a number of options are possible to answer this question. The quantitative interpretation to representativeness proposes to use random sampling (or stratified sampling) as the best option. This is not the appropriate methodological device in the case of Rapid Appraisal as its purpose is to understand the experience of living in a community, and the perceptions of priority needs flowing from that experience. Qualitative approaches are targeted at exploring experiential issues, and rely on purposive sampling, that is, selecting specific cases (individuals or groups) which are representative of the various perspectives within the sample population. In the Rapid Appraisal this can be approached in a number of ways: if previous knowledge exists about the community, and the different subgroups within it, a matrix of possible cases for inclusion can be drawn up. For example, in one community epidemiological and service usage data revealed the existence of a large number of people over 65 of which a proportion were suffering from specific conditions, a concentration of young single mothers, a number of drug users, a defined percentage of unemployed people in particular pockets and so on. Combining locality and interest groups together allowed a clear set of characteristics to be defined for the cases to be included in the Rapid Appraisal fieldwork interviews.

The other axis against which sampling has to be measured concerns perceptions and interpretations. Divisions within a community as outlined above are experienced in different ways, and if one is not using a random sampling methodology, it is important in terms of validity to ascertain the fullest possible range of perspectives. Concretely, the experience of being an old person in a community can be explored from the viewpoint of elderly people themselves, but also from that of providers of services (both formal and informal) and those who plan services. Furthermore, community leaders (appointed or self-appointed) possess generalized and accumulated knowledge about this particular subgroup. It is precisely these differences that Rapid Appraisal exploits, and attempts to create a bridge between universal understanding of need – through comparative, epidemiological and other methods – and the diversity of need as expressed by different groupings within communities.

Translating these ideas into practice, Rapid Appraisals do not access the community through random sampling, but use the purposive method by selecting specific individuals and groups for in-depth interviews. They can be broadly divided into three categories:

1. People who are at the centre of social networks and have 'their finger on the pulse', understanding particular subsets of the community or interest groups. These people are, for example, shop owners, librarians, traffic wardens and voluntary workers.

2. People who are considered to be community leaders, either elected such as members of parliament, or informally elected such as church leaders and chairmen of pressure groups.

3. People who work in the community (but not necessarily live there) and through their work have knowledge of particular

problems or subgroups, such as teachers, social workers, General Practitioners or dentists.

In Chapter 6 the actual data collection and analysis and the ways in which the various perspectives will be compared will be discussed. The issue here is that the community is defined in research terms through a 'proxy' method, that is to collect material about the experience of living within a particular community through a careful matching of perspectives. This first stage of data gathering for a needs profile does not preclude the involvement of the total community at subsequent stages. The second stage of prioritization can, for example, be extended beyond the small group of 50 respondents and include a larger number of stakeholders, or the whole community. An example of the latter can be found in Dallam, Warrington (Snee, 1991) where a group of community members developed a questionnaire which they themselves administered to the community. Another alternative is to develop an initial priority listing and go to the community for a poll on the key priorities.

Rapid Appraisal is not a static methodology and allows for innovation and variation on its themes. Certainly, the question of community involvement can be tackled in a number of ways involving different sections of the community, or the whole community, at different stages in the process. The main injunction is to assess the validity of the findings in a rigorous manner, and a constant feedback loop into the community is a key device alongside the comparative analysis of the qualitative and quantitative material. Creating a broad-based acceptance of the findings of a Rapid Appraisal through the involvement of key individuals and groups within the community is important for building up relationships between communities and policy-makers, as this has to be the starting point for formulating strategy and policy in a participatory manner.

An example of the people included in the community interviews in Woodforde:

1. people at the centre of social networks: hairdresser, shop keeper, milkman, publican, rugby club, teenage group;

2. leaders in the community: District Councillor, Community Association secretary, Chair of West Indian Association (and other ethnic minority groups), Convenor of Residents' Association;

3. professionals: police, head of school, GP, warden of elderly people's home, vet, caretaker of primary school, special needs school staff, community centre staff.

The practical consideration precluding a randomized approach is time. Random sampling in a community of 10 000–12 000 people results in a sample size of at least 200 cases. Qualitative interviews (or at the minimum semi-structured interviews) would be extremely time-consuming with such a large sample, and the rapidity of Rapid Appraisal would soon dissipate. Thus, a purposive sample, with clearly circumscribed sample characteristics can be drawn up and not exceed 50 cases.

<table><tr><td>**4**</td><td># Power, knowledge and health policy</td></tr></table>

Community involvement is based upon the notion of empowerment, which presupposes an understanding of the form and nature of power in the health policy process. Health policy can be regarded as a process involving a series of more or less related activities and their intended and unintended consequences for those concerned (Walt, 1994). Furthermore, health policy is generally considered to operate on two levels, as macro policy at the level of national or regional government, or as micro policy at the district or institutional level. In this book the concern is mainly with micro level policy, as this is the environment within which communities can make their interventions, and Rapid Appraisal can be most effective. It has been argued that, at the micro level, policy-making is more likely to be pluralist; that is, to allow the expression of different interests, and therefore, challenging vested interests which in this case are held by the medical profession and health care managers. Barrett and McMahon (1990) also state that at the micro level the policy process is characterized by the interaction between policy-making and policy implementation.

In this chapter these two themes are explored when discussing the various forms of power and their knowledge base. The medical scientific paradigm, scientific managerialism and lay knowledge will be discussed and the ways in which they can be juxtaposed in order to clarify the relations of power in the health policy process. Different models of power will be presented in order to set a framework for understanding the boundaries of methods used to empower communities. The emphasis of Rapid Appraisal is on policy implementation, and thus the analysis of power and the negotiation of power relationships is central to understanding the interaction between policy formulation and its implementation. The key issue is whether lay knowledge can offer a convincing challenge to both medical and managerial knowledge, and be inserted as a valid paradigm within the decision-making process.

WHICH PARADIGM?

The medical profession has been a fascinating subject of study for social scientists notably because it offers a key case study of power (Freidson, 1970, 1988). From this starting point medicine has been analysed in a number of different ways, including its role in preserving the capitalist order (Navarro, 1978), the way in which medicine inculcates its own culture into those entering the profession, thus perpetuating its own discourse (Becker, 1961), the professionalization and de-professionalization question (Larson, 1977), and many other issues which have been recently reviewed by Kelleher, Gabe and Williams (1994). Here, the focus is on how the medical scientific paradigm as a body of knowledge dominates the definition of health needs and outcomes, and the way in which this way of thinking has been challenged by the scientific management paradigm on the one hand, and lay knowledge on the other hand.

In most Western countries the scientific medical model has been dominant and powerful, and determined the shape of health policy and institutions. While many authors have questioned the reductionist approach, exemplified in the engineering model (McKeown, 1976), or doubted its effectiveness in curing disease, and instead creating more (Illich, 1975), in essence, medicine remains rooted in a natural science base. This foundation is most clearly demonstrated in the methods adopted by medical science, namely the reliance on experimental designs. The randomized controlled trial (RCT) is considered to be the gold standard for scientific proof (Pope and Mays, 1993), whilst in reality only a minority of accepted medical interventions have been subject to rigorous RCT testing. Yet, the RCT is a powerful element in the medical folklore, emphasizing its technicality and reliance on robust evidence.

However, medicine is full of uncertainty, be it uncertainty about the aetiology of diseases, effective treatments or outcomes in individuals. On the one hand, medicine evokes the image of controlling disease by offering a cure, based on scientific rationality and evidence, on the other hand, it is continually faced with old and newly emerging uncertainties. Breast cancer represents a clear case of continual uncertainty, lack of progress in the treatment, and women turning to other healing paradigms. The discovery of HIV and AIDS symbolizes the type of new uncertainty that poses a dilemma for the scientific method as the complex disease pattern, the social correlates and individual behaviour defy clear predictions about the progress of the disease in individuals. On the other hand, medicine can be considered to be an 'art', with knowledge lodged within the individual practitioner who has learned through experience. This conceptualization of medicine emphasizes the power of the medical 'gaze' (Foucault, 1973) which serves to redefine the patient, and expropriate the person's own definition of self, and his or her experience of illness. The interpretation of symptoms into a medical diagnosis and appropriate treatment is the prerogative of the doctor, and as Jamous and Peloille (1970) argue, this indeterminacy retains the mystique of medicine.

Medicine is centrally concerned with disease, whereby disease is understood to be a pathological condition recognized by indications, such as signs and symptoms, agreed among biomedical practitioners (Helman, 1985; Stacey, 1988). Disease as a biological or clinically defined abnormality is a reductionist concept, and divides psyche and soma. The successes of scientific medicine cannot be underestimated, such as for example, surgical developments which have now been revolutionized with minimal access techniques. Conversely, the limits to medicine have become more obvious, and progress has sometimes been attributed to medicine, whilst the true origins lie outside it, such as improvements in water and sanitation, or socio-economic conditions (exemplified in inequalities in health between different socio-economic groupings, Cox *et al.*, 1993). Most importantly, the emphasis on disease excludes the perceptions of the sufferer. The distinction between disease and illness helps to understand the conceptual distinction, whereby illness is defined as the subjective state which is experienced by the individual. This experience is influenced by social and cultural notions about illness, and some argue that it should be broadened out to the experience of disorder (Locker, 1981) thus allowing individuals to decide whether they suffer from illness which requires a medical intervention, or whether their illness remains outside the medical paradigm.

Medical values derived from the scientific model reflect its individualistic bias, taking the sufferer out of context and reducing him or her to a set of symptoms. Taussig (1980) calls this process the reification of the body, which has continued with the advent of new technologies such as mediating the vision of the body through endoscopic projection of internal images outside the body (Ong, 1993). The patient is drawn into the realm of medical definitions, and the experiential aspects of illness do not sit comfortably within this frame of reference. The power of the medical view is reinforced by the social beliefs that medicine and its practitioners work for the good of the patient, and that determining the appropriateness and quality of care are the prerogative of medicine. In spite of those views coming under increasing pressure, the status of the medical profession continues to be high in most Western societies, and confidence in doctors' decisions about care remains strong. The implication for health policy is that the medical perspective remains a powerful determinant in the assessment of needs and priorities. Yet, this power is increasingly under threat, and medical hegemony has been questioned both from within the health care sector and from alternative medical models (Kelleher, Gabe and Williams, 1994). The threats that are most relevant within the context of this discussion are those from the managerial and the lay perspectives, which each offer a contrasting paradigm.

In the 1980s and 1990s the majority of Western developed countries have instigated health sector reform. The reasons behind the reforms are various and complex, and appear to be more fundamental than those carried out in the previous decades. Despite social, economic and cultural differences the objectives of the reforms demonstrate similarities in objectives, notably the drive to control public expenditure, and health and social care spending in particular. Many countries have opted for a (quasi) market orientation, and competition is seen as a vehicle for driving the reforms in the organization and environment of health care (Ham, 1993a; May, 1994; Poullier, 1994). One of the key factors in pushing through reforms – and in certain countries the pace of reforms is fast – is the development of management in order to deliver the objectives of the reforms.

In the case of Great Britain, the foundations for reform, and the attendant development of management was laid in 1983 with the Griffiths proposal (Griffiths, 1983). The history and principles behind the subsequent reforms have been reviewed by other authors (e.g. Strong and Robinson, 1990; Harrison *et al.*, 1992; Pettigrew *et al.*, 1992; Ham, 1994). Instead we will focus on the development of management as an alternative source of power within health policy-making.

Unlike medicine, management does not have a strict disciplinary foundation, and instead draws on a variety of disciplines such as for example psychology and sociology, in order to construct a coherent approach to the management enterprise and its analysis. Flynn (1992) traces the origins of scientific management back to Taylorism in the USA in 1911, which refers to a set of ideas about organizational design and manager–employee relations within a capitalist context. He goes on to state that scientific management deliberately fragments the division of labour and separates planning from the process of production. In this way management is depicted as a specialized activity affording managers the right to co-ordinate and command workers. This leads Flynn to draw the parallel with the health care sector where 'scientific management is regarded as a generic movement comprising a number of interrelated aspects. Its main aim is to increase workers' productivity, and remove workers' craft control of the work process by vesting power in managers and in the production arrangements themselves' (p.32). Leaving the treatment of the concept of power until later in this chapter it is necessary to examine whether management constitutes a paradigm which differs fundamentally from the medical model.

The development of management as a science stimulated different schools of thought with the human relations school (Roethlisberger and Dickson, 1939; MacGregor, 1960) offering a contrasting perspective from Taylor by focusing on the way people performed and accomplished tasks. The emphasis shifted to understanding the formal and informal structures of organizations, and thus to the management of people and their relationships. In recent years this approach led to an interest in culture and leadership in organizations (Peters and

Waterman, 1982). A further theoretical body of work was developed by the proponents of systems theory, a catch-all for a number of different strands, but with a unifying emphasis on the holistic nature of organizations and the importance of synergy (Senge, 1992). The latter two approaches have found resonance in shifting the emphasis from productivity and competitive edge towards delegation and participation, or in the current parlance, the formulation of an organization's mission from the bottom-up.

Commentators (Parston, 1993) have labelled the recent shift the 'new management' which is characterized by concepts such as communication, collaboration, emotion and win–win situations. While this may be dismissed as a new jargon, it does constitute a departure from the previous paradigms, and significantly within the context of the discussion in this chapter, sets it apart from the medical paradigm, which reflects individualism, hierarchy, detachment and esoteric knowledge. Apart from the difference in theoretical orientation it can be argued that public sector managers have to recognize the demands of the policy environment and the way it affects their capacity to deliver organizational objectives. This places particular pressures on the new management paradigm, because the health of a country's economy largely determines the way in which there is managerial freedom in the public sector to experiment with more liberal organizational forms.

Research carried out on different forms of managerial leadership has thrown an interesting light on the above problem. Rosener (1990) examined male and female leadership styles in organizations and concluded that interactive approaches – often associated with women –which include sharing of power and information, motivating others, charismatic leadership and flexibility, offer more scope for organizational survival in a competitive and diverse economic environment. These conclusions can be equally applied to the health sector, where the creativity of many professionals as a corporate whole provide a valuable mix of expertise, and the flux of health reform has created a multitude of situations where a blue-print management style would not provide the answers. It is argued that a flexible, creative approach to management will be able to respond to the uniqueness of each organization, and thus facilitates responsiveness to change. In short, the management paradigm is now characterized by an eclectic and fluid approach, which is required to be infinitely adaptable to both the pressure of the broader policy environment, and the contradictions from within the health sector. This does not, however, negate the need for management to maintain control over the processes of production, as the organizational objectives remain to be fulfilled. The tension between the purpose and form of management is one which poses a number of conflicts between the medical and managerial models, and we will return to this question when discussing the question of power.

The third body of knowledge which needs to be examined here is the lay paradigm. Perhaps, it is an overstatement to call this a paradigm, as it contains a diversity of world views. Yet, we will focus on the common foundation of lay knowledge, and draw on the analysis of Williams and Popay (1994a) who build on predominantly sociological and anthropological work on the nature of lay knowledge. The clear distinction between disease as physiological and clinical abnormality, and illness as the subjective experience of the sufferer (Helman, 1985) has already been referred to, but signifies the conceptual gap between the medical and lay paradigms. In focusing on the cultural and social specificity of the illness experience, it is possible to uncover the multiple interpretations that can be attached to one disease, thus illuminating the various possible responses to diagnosis and treatment. Taking this one step further, Williams and Popay argue that the recognition of lay knowledge permits a proper understanding of health problems, thus posing an *epistemological* (authors' emphasis) challenge to expert knowledge. They go on to say that lay knowledge also poses a *political* (authors' emphasis) challenge to the institutional power of experts, and in particular, medical knowledge because it questions the authority of professionals as the only experts to define problems in the policy arena. This argument can be extended to the relationship between lay and managerial knowledge. The managerial paradigm focuses on interpretation of disease patterns in order to formulate an organizational response within the confines of policy objectives of efficiency, effectiveness and prioritization. Thus, it tends to be interested in the professional assessment of disease categories and service responses, and at an organizational level can only partially respond to the diversity of individual experience.

Precisely because of the kaleidoscopic nature of illness experiences, lay knowledge has been marginalized by medicine and management alike as subjective, idiosyncratic and representing 'soft' evidence. However, the activities of many self-help groups in the 1980s and 1990s have offered a counter critique by complementing the technical–instrumental definitions of medicine and management through expressing 'life-world' concerns (Kelleher, 1994) that can be translated into practical needs of specific groups or individuals. The women's movement's analysis and efforts to change the orientation of professionals and services engaged in pregnancy and childbirth is one of the most celebrated examples (Oakley, 1980). It can, however, be argued that those examples have been confined to particular areas of the health care enterprise, but not fundamentally altered the medical and management paradigms. Kuhn's (1970) proposition, that paradigmatic change only happens when the existing paradigm has ceased to explain adequately the phenomena which are the focus of the application of that paradigm, is relevant in this discussion. While the lay perspective poses a challenge to both the medical and managerial bodies of knowledge, the question remains as to how big a challenge it is. Kuhn states that not only the impact of the nature and the logic of the alternative paradigm has to be examined, but also the techniques of persuasive argumentation that are required within each scientific community to effect change. The foundation of lay knowledge lies in the individual narrative, which displays an internal coherence, and often reflects scientific medical concepts, yet, precisely because it is individually-based penetration into either the medical or managerial community, becomes fragmented and difficult to achieve. In order to assess the possibilities of mutuality of paradigms, we have to engage in a discussion of power.

MODELS OF POWER AND THE POWER OF LAY KNOWLEDGE

The most commonly used framework for analysing power is the one formulated by Lukes (1974) which outlines three dimensions of power. The first dimension refers to an observable situation in which there is overt conflict between individuals or groups, and whereby the dominant party controls the situation, thus protecting its own dominance. The second dimension of power occurs in situations where there is covert as well as overt conflict between two parties, but the subordinate party decides not to act as it perceives itself to be in a losing position. This means that the dominant group retains its dominance without having to act. It is particularly the discovery of the third face of power which made Lukes' analysis attractive as it examines the invisible way in which power permeates consciousness. Precisely, because the dominant party actually exercizes its power by influencing, shaping or determining the wants of the subordinate party, it has total control over the thought processes of the latter. Hugman (1991) considers the contribution of the third dimension to lie in its recognition of the social nature of the action on which power is focused, including both the 'power over' and the 'power to' act. Harrison *et al.* (1992) review the objections against Lukes's position and state that as there are no observable conflicts of values, no observable exercising of power takes place. However, they go on to argue, that if the dominant party acknowledges that it actually does attempt to shape the subordinate party's values, the issue would be different. Harrison *et al.* illustrate this with the case of modification of organizational cultures in the NHS.

Recently, a different critique has been voiced about the Lukes model, emphasizing its limitations because it is rooted in a conflict model of power, and therefore does not allow sufficient explanation for the complexity of relationships, contingencies and the latent operation of power. Cooper (1994) argues that wants and needs are socially constructed, and she objects to Lukes' a-historical interpretation of wants existing as objective entities, outside social relationships. She draws on Foucault (1978) when arguing that Lukes attempts to find conflict in situations where it is not apparent. In doing so, he does not recognize that conflict can be minimized or removed through the construction of shared knowledge, desires, interests and values. In contrast, Cooper reconceptualizes power 'as the production, facilitation or maintenance of particular outcomes, processes or social relations. In this way, power does not have inevitable negative connotations. Whether it operates in a progressive or reactionary way depends on its form, the terrains on which it operates, and on the nature of those exercising and subject to power within a given social and historical moment' (p.452).

The above analysis opens the way for looking at power as, on the one hand, potential or actual conflict, or on the other hand, as a mechanism to manage meaning and to create legitimacy of certain forms of knowledge (Eden, 1989). The latter approach links with the literature on ideology, where power is seen to shape rules, practices and procedures which are perceived as the natural order. Rather than elaborating on this theoretical body of knowledge, the avenue explored here is the way in which resources can be used to operate as modes of power in order to create advantage, be it material or otherwise. This is expressed within a health context as, for example, rights to practise, monopoly over skills, access to specific technical materials and so on. The application of those resources perpetuates specific power relations, and for the subordinate or excluded group, sharing power becomes difficult.

Our concern here is with the relations of power between the medical profession, managers and the public, and particularly the way in which the lay perspective can open up professional (medical and managerial) dominance. In the British context the balance of power between doctors and managers has been an area of investigation ever since the introduction of general management (Griffiths, 1983). In analysing the development and operation of scientific management in the British NHS Flynn argues that the dominance of the medical profession has been eroded by the combined forces of government intervention (i.e. the nature and pace of the reforms) and managerial power. Accountability of doctors has become transformed into corporate accountability, and the proliferation of tools measuring performance in audit and monitoring can be seen as key devices through which medicine is being controlled by management bureaucracies. Yet, the degree to which medical power has been significantly reduced remains open to debate, and others have argued that it is too early to gauge accurately.

Hunter (1991, 1994) cites both US and British experiences where managerial dominance at the expense of doctors have failed, and had to be adapted in order to avoid confrontation. The trend of involving doctors in management has gathered momentum, but Hunter feels that it is less clear what the form and nature of doctors' involvement will take. Current studies on clinicians' involvement in managing acute services (Boaden *et al.*, 1995) indicate that models are still evolving, and doctors continue to inhabit the terrain between medicine and management. Innovators, product champions and early adopters (Stocking, 1984) of general management in medicine are shifting the foundation of their power to budget holding, corporate and departmental decision-making; late adopters see their power base to lie in professional categories such as medical excellence. However, this division is not as clear-cut as it seems, with doctors balancing the managerial and medical yardsticks alongside each other, and the way in which legitimacy is defined will determine the power base of the profession. Different scenarios can, therefore, be constructed. For example, doctors can use managerial paradigms to strengthen their own knowledge base by integrating managerial concepts into their everyday medical discourse. The introduction of minimal access techniques offers an interesting illustration: their practical adoption has been determined by cost reduction and higher throughput of patients rather than by randomized controlled trials (the clinical gold standard). The effect, however, is that medical knowledge and decision-making has been reinforced rather than diluted.

Hunter (1994) also considers that the social status of doctors has not fundamentally diminished and the 'collusive relationship with the public (...) has allowed medicine's conception of health and disease to remain dominant' (p.17). Challenges to doctors' power as exemplified in the growing number of complaints and litigations, have not necessarily meant an erosion of the power of the profession, rather a questioning of the competence of individual practitioners. Taking these various arguments together, the outcome of the medicine–management interface is far from clear, and the continued support of the public for the medical profession appears to maintain the balance tipped in favour of doctors.

The managerial–lay interface has undergone some interesting changes. In many Western developed countries users of health services have become more informed, articulate in their demands and want to influence policy. Examples of this trend have already been mentioned, but the fact that they tend to be confined to specific interest groups and affect only a small part of health services, has meant that neither medical or managerial power has been significantly eroded. In Britain, like in many other countries, policy initiatives have been designed to involve the public in health policy, predominantly at local levels. The British variant is entitled 'Local Voices' requiring purchasers of health care to base their decisions on knowledge of people's perceptions, preferences and experience of health services. Health authorities, as purchasers of care, must try to establish local legitimacy for their priorities. They must also consider consultation seriously and be open-minded and receptive (Mawhinney, 1994). This may appear a laudable initiative but it tends to overlook major structural weaknesses. If power is perceived as creating legitimacy using particular resources such as specialist skills, information, materials, access and so on, local people are not in any way equal players in the power game. Furthermore, actual accountability to local communities has been gradually eroded in Britain with representation on health authorities and trusts being reduced to centrally appointed non-executive directors and the removal of local authority representatives – and the Community Health Councils a few years earlier. Without controlling social vectors essential to exercising power the Local Voices idea looks more like a hollow slogan, covering up the lack of power that the lay perspective can wield. A more fundamental review of the ways in which knowledge becomes legitimated is required, and where lay knowledge can be inserted to actually change the face of power.

CHANGING KNOWLEDGE

The limitations of medical knowledge have been explored by social scientists and anthropologists in particular, who have pointed out that scientific medicine cannot explain the experience of illness (Comaroff and Maguire, 1981), and have provided evidence of the contradictions within the scientific paradigm itself (Richman, 1987). The most important feature in this work has been the insistence that medicine cannot divorce itself from its cultural context and maintain its stance of being value-free. In particular, inter-group and inter-individual variations can be traced back to different cultural experiences alongside differences in clinical pathology. This implies that in understanding this diversity, the lay perspective has to be inserted, and valued on its own terms rather than being expropriated through medical reformulation of symptoms and experience. Williams and Popay (1994a) argue that lay perspectives on health and illness are infinitely complex, and display internal coherence and validity in terms of the purpose they fulfil for the person who holds them. Rather than dismissing this knowledge as idiosyncratic and irrelevant, medicine can be enriched by linking its search for classification and precision in labelling disease categories with the lay focus on the experience of the impact of disease and making sense of disease within the personal history and narrative logic. Lay knowledge transforms then from being an impediment to understanding causality, the course and impact of disease, to an essential ingredient in the diagnosis and treatment of disease. In Cooper's (1994) definition of power this integration offers new avenues for the production, facilitation or maintenance of particular health outcomes, processes and practices which are defined by both doctors and users of services.

The idea of integrating perspectives is perhaps not as far fetched as would have been thought a decade ago. In Britain doctors are now contemplating revisiting the 'core values' of their profession. This has happened as a result of combined pressures from government, managers and the public – and has found its parallel in many other developed countries. In effect, the three-way interface between medicine, management and public has forced doctors to evaluate their knowledge and value base. The interim outcome of the British debate resulted in an emphasis on six core values: caring, integrity, competence, confidentiality, responsibility and advocacy (Smith, 1994).

The first impression is that these values represent the three perspectives, for example, the concept of caring must be influenced by lay perspectives as it needs to encompass cultural perceptions of caring (Finch, 1989) and the holistic experience of health care. The convergence of medical and managerial perspectives can be read into the value of competence which goes beyond the traditional clinical expertise, but embraces concern with clinical standards, outcomes, effectiveness, audit and the ability to define outcomes (Calman, 1994). The realization that priority-setting and choices, negotiation and understanding the policy process has taken root in the medical profession and a reframing of conceptual concepts has begun, born from the need to understand the longer-term effects of managerialism in the health service. Following on from Hunter's analysis of power it is, as yet, uncertain whether medical knowledge has been irrevocably changed by incorporating managerial frameworks, or whether these can be absorbed in the dominant paradigm of medicine.

The relationship between lay knowledge and scientific managerialism is less well documented, but a number of trends can be detected. Health policy in many developed countries is increasingly centred around organizational and financial reform symbolized in a number of key issues such as defining health gain (Welsh Office, 1989; Department of Health, 1992), necessary care (Dunning, 1992) and quality (Maxwell, 1984; Hopkins and Maxwell, 1990). These issues, and many others, can be clarified by the lay perspective. For example, the concept of health incorporates many cultural notions of normality and citizen's aspirations. Equally, the term necessary care is predicated upon a clear understanding of a community's or society's perceptions of participation in order sufficiently to achieve the identity as a social being. Quality is in the eye of the beholder, and thus requires the subject of care to define the concept in order to counterbalance professional and managerial notions.

Shifting the basis and boundaries of knowledge is a difficult enterprise as it encounters resistance from powerful interest groups. Yet, the degree of uncertainty evoked by the momentous changes in health policy and health care across many developed countries can create a context in which these shifts can be accelerated. It requires clarity of purpose to recognize the opportunities which exist in opening up bodies of knowledge to the influences of alternative paradigms. At the macro level an overarching research-based vision could affect Foucault's idea of the productive aspects of power to come to fruition by clarifying the objectives for the various stakeholders, and providing the broad knowledge base for the achievement of these objectives. At the micro level the less powerful groups of patients and users have to simultaneously be supported to voice their perspective as a legitimate source of knowledge and expertise within the overall scientific analysis of health and health care.

Questions of power in Rapid Appraisal

Rapid Appraisal fundamentally questions the knowledge base and the sources of power of decision-makers. By focusing on the community perspective the knowledge lodged within communities is made visible and validated. Moreover, the methodological approach adopted within Rapid Appraisal is eclectic, and incorporates both quantitative (for example, census, survey and epidemiological data) with qualitative methods (for example, observation, ethnographic interviews). Williams and Popay (1994a) argue clearly that understanding the nature of lay knowledge demands an egalitarian approach. The methods used should be able to uncover the individual or group narrative, that is being able to put people's experiences within a historical and socio-cultural context. Therefore, unstructured interviews are most suited to this type of inquiry. This does not mean that the researcher does not know what to ask, rather that within a broad thematic approach the respondent is encouraged to tell their own story, following their own logic – oral history, critical incidence techniques and so on. The assumption is that there is not one truth, rather there are multiple truths which taken together provide the rich tapestry of people's lives and the place of health within their consciousness and daily existence. This knowledge is therefore equally valid and important as the medical, managerial or other professional perspectives.

Rapid Appraisal considers the notion of empowerment as central to its philosophy. This is not a unitary concept and encompasses a range of meanings: a patient's choice of a specific provider, influence over treatment modalities, control over budgetary allocations or elections for health-related politicians (Saltman, 1992). The origins of empowerment also differ: in a conflict model power can be wrested from the powerful, in a productive model power can be shared. Despite these variations it can be assumed that those in power are not easily giving up power, and even if they are inclined to do so, the change of consciousness required often represents a giant leap.

In a sense Rapid Appraisal can be considered a top-down initiative which constitutes both its strength and its weakness. Because it is top-down, Rapid Appraisal is concerned with real power. At the same time the parameters for sharing power tend to be defined by the powerful, who potentially can limit the genuine shift in power. It can be argued that this is always the case, whoever instigates the change. In the Rapid Appraisal this is explicit, and the initiators of the exercise have to be clear about their objectives and their own motives. More importantly, they have to be reflective and assess whether they will cope with fundamental challenges to their body of knowledge and other sources of power. To some extent this is an academic exercise, and the proof of the pudding is in the eating, yet, at the start of a Rapid Appraisal exercise the discussion of power has to be entered into, and people need to be aware of the personal or corporate discomfort that will be experienced in the process.

A further issue which has particularly arisen in the British context is the question of who should be part of the Rapid Appraisal team. In theory, the assessment of community needs and perspectives is the remit of purchasers. In practice, they represent only one body of knowledge, that is scientific managerialism, and the professional perspective (health, social, education, housing, etc.) is vested in providers. If Rapid Appraisal is to open up theoretical paradigms the participation of purchasers and providers is crucial. Furthermore, the understanding of the lay perspective is equally different from a purchaser or provider point of view, with the former focusing on general or client populations, and the latter on individuals and client populations. For the communities participating in a Rapid Appraisal the dialogue with both sets of stakeholders is fruitful as they will gain insight in the different logics and modes of decision-making, and therefore, strengthen their own strategies for dealing with these powerful groupings.

In practice, most Rapid Appraisals have enlisted purchasers and providers in their teams. This has, apart from the above presumed opportunities, the unintended programme effect of providing a further platform for dialogue between purchasers and providers. The discussions on the challenges to power, and the limits to empowerment have to be engaged in from the start and continued throughout the process, both within the Rapid Appraisal team, and with the communities concerned. Only if this is carried out in a transparent manner can the Rapid Appraisal gain credibility as an attempt to question power and knowledge. The way in which policy can then be reframed is a topic which will be addressed in Chapter 7.

Examples of team compositions

Team 1
Deputy Housing Officer.
Director of Nursing (Community Health Unit).
Director of Planning (Community Health Unit).
Director of Nursing Services (Mental Health Unit).
Head of Health Promotion (Health Authority).
Assistant Chief Executive (Family Health Service Authority – primary care).
Clinical Psychologist – Health Promotion.
Manager of Research and Development (Community Health Unit).
Area Manager (Social Services).
Manager of Research (Social Services)

Team 2
Chief Executive (Family Health Services Authority).
Director of Public Health (Commission).
Director of Environmental Health and Leisure (District Council).
Principal Projects Advisor (District Council).
Head of Information Services (County Council).
Primary Care Manager (Health Commission).
District Social Care Manager (Social Services).
Service Specification Manager (Public Health Department).
Locality Manager (Community Health Trust).
Patient Care Manager (Hospital Trust).
Town Council representative.

<table>
<tr><td>**5**</td><td># Whose priorities?</td></tr>
</table>

The reality of unlimited health need and demand for care versus limited resources, which prevails in most countries of the world, presents the making of choices and setting of priorities as an inevitability in health policy. This chapter will address the question of priorities, starting with a discussion of the notion of priority within a broader social and policy context. The debate as to whether priorities can be defined in a rational scientific manner, or whether they are essentially value-laden is considered to be central, and necessary for addressing the second area. This is concerned with a brief overview of methodologies, and the way in which they represent rational models, or are based upon 'social utility' concepts (Maynard, 1994). The third question to be addressed focuses on the role of communities in priority-setting: why should they be involved, and if so, how? Who represents the community views, and what methods are available to tap those views? The fourth question focuses on the problem of the structure of decision-making in health policy and whether accountability and transparency of choices can be realized. Achieving change is directly related to these issues, and influences the way in which the cycle of 'needs–priorities–interventions–outcomes' can be closed.

Rapid Appraisal has the intention to make the process of priority-setting explicit by involving communities as equal partners with professionals, and comparing the different priority listings. At the same time, a number of the above-mentioned issues are less clearly addressed, such as the basis on which choices are made (if one presumes that the value judgements of professionals and communities differ), whether the method within Rapid Appraisal is sufficiently sophisticated to embrace the widest possible range of preferences, and how accountability for choices is established. In the final part of this chapter we will attempt to answer these questions, and provide some examples of priority listings within Rapid Appraisal.

WHY PRIORITIES?

Priority-setting is not new, and has been done in many health care systems

(Ham, 1993b). In the literature the notions of priority-setting and rationing are inextricably linked, and economists consider them synonymous, which means that the terms are often used interchangeably. However, rationing is considered to be an emotive term while priority-setting has the aura of being more objective. In this chapter we will not make a clear distinction between the two, as the processes cannot be divorced from each other.

Harrison and Hunter (1994) state that rationing has to take place in any health care system where services are not paid directly by the user because there is a tendency for user demands to increase where services are perceived to be free and good for them. Thus, the assumption upon which priority-setting is based is on what Maynard (1994) calls one of the certainties in life: the scarcity of resources. The realization that resources are scarce has to be confronted in both the developed and developing world, and a number of factors have emphasized this, such as the world-wide cost inflation associated with economic recession, the developments in medical technologies and the widespread acceptance of many (sometimes unproven) techniques, the ageing of populations and so on. As a result, the pressures upon health care systems are increasing, and the inevitability of making choices in how to use available resources has to be accepted. Green and Barker (1988) argue that a narrow focus on priority-setting in health care risks losing sight of the processes determining health, which demand a holistic perspective on making choices in a wider arena of social life. This point will be elaborated upon when discussing the various techniques used for priority-setting, but it is important to emphasize this issue. It tends to be based upon a medical model of determining parameters, while a concern with health demands the inclusion of social and lay models, and furthermore, requires one to ponder on the question of how equity and setting priorities can be reconciled.

When comparing the experiences in different countries and different systems, the emphasis appears to be on how to set priorities, rather than to whether priorities should be set. The latter consideration tends to be accepted *a priori* partly because it is seen to be unavoidable (Dunning, 1992; Harrison and Hunter, 1994) and partly because it has always been practised implicitly through, for example, the operation of waiting lists. The main difference is that the discussion has now become explicit, predominantly because of the major structural changes that are taking place in many health systems. The emergence of quasi-markets in Britain (Paton, 1993) and many other Western countries, and the creation of the role of purchaser (or commissioner) of health care has meant that implicit, and clinician-based priority-setting should be transformed to explicit, purchaser-based decision-making. In reality, these two models operate in parallel, but the individual-oriented clinical choices are intended to be progressively phased out.

The setting of priorities in health has firstly, tended to focus mainly on health and medical care and secondly, been concerned with models and techniques which assisted in establishing the choices as rational. The emphasis on clinical interventions originates from the dominance of scientific medical thinking in most health systems, and the belief that the contribution of medical treatment can be measured. Measurement is primarily carried out through employing models that collect and analyse apparently objective and quantifiable data on outcomes resulting from specific interventions. The time horizon of these measurements has to be relatively short in order to be useful for health planning, and as a result, most effort has been expended in acute and secondary care, rather than in primary and community care. The latter two sectors pose a number of problems, notably, the blurring of boundaries between prevention and treatment, and treatment and rehabilitation or continuing care. Furthermore, the contribution of sectors other than health, and in particular, the informal (community) sector of care cannot be easily measured. The theoretical and philosophical difficulties have not been addressed systematically by most researchers, and as Green and Barker (1988) argue, this has led to a focus on models and techniques which move away from the Primary Health Care approach as defined by the WHO. The holistic concept of health is consequently undermined by the emphasis on disease-based outcome measures, leading to vertical programmes, and reinforcing the power of planning bureaucracies to influence heavily, if not determine, priorities (p.922). The key charge against the so-called rational models is that their value base is obscured in the same way as quantitative methods purport to be neutral and value free. In the realm of social problems – and priority-setting can be considered as such – value free solutions by means of the application of science do not exist, because science itself is socially constructed, and thus embodies certain social values about rationality and evidence (McKeown *et al.*, 1994). It is, therefore, important to review briefly some of the key approaches in order to assess these arguments, and to provide a background against which Rapid Appraisal can be placed as an alternative method.

PRIORITY-SETTING METHODS

Scientific merit of health interventions – traditionally decided upon by individual clinicians – cannot alone be sufficient in priority-setting; issues such as cost-effectiveness, social and ethical implications must also be included. Difficult decisions have to be made daily, and Maynard (1994) argues that the tools for making those decisions have advanced relatively little over the last decade. However, the body of knowledge which has increasingly been used, despite its shortcomings, is economic appraisal.

A fundamental criterium in selecting a particular course of action is: what are the costs of taking this action? From the economist's point of view 'costs' mean 'what will have to be sacrificed?' (Williams, F., 1992), that is, what is the cost and resource usage in comparison to the next best alternative. The sacrifice tends not to be viewed at the individual level, but at the population level. The other part of the equation is that a measure of possible benefit has to be constructed. One of the most widely discussed measures is the Quality Adjusted Life Year (QALY) (Williams, A., 1985). The QALY's use in prioritization is based upon the assumption that a year of life is of equal value to everyone, regardless of age or other factors; that it is specific to the patient alone and that values obtained may be aggregated across individuals. The QALY is an index that allows a trade-off for length and quality of life to be combined into a single health state valuation and which places eight states of disability and four states of distress into a composite index. Using values between 1 (perfectly healthy) to 0 (dead) the QALY provides an index for comparison and consequently, prioritization (Kind *et al.*, 1982; Gudex and Kind, 1987).

A range of criticisms have been levelled at the QALY, including technical inadequacies (Donaldson *et al.*, 1988), limitations in its application (Donaldson, 1989) and theoretical objections concerning whether the value judgements involved in applying relative weights to different dimensions of health, can actually be organized into a technical framework, and applied *a priori* (Carr-Hill, 1991). Conversely, the argument could be made that a common index offers the opportunity to compare health interventions (Williams, A., 1989), and provides decision-makers with a common currency for deciding on priorities (Williams, A., 1988; Hadorn, 1991). Interestingly, Williams points out that an effectiveness measure such as the QALY tends to be seen as the appropriate *technical* (original emphasis) way of doing things, and that the implicit value judgement is often not recognized (1992, p.9). This statement relates closely to the question posed by Green and Barker who insist that it is important to establish *who* (original emphasis) makes the assessment (1988, p.926). An answer to this question can help to open up decision-making within the measurement process and create a space for alternative modes of assessment involving communities.

The second, and equally well publicized method of priority-setting is the one adopted by the state of Oregon. The historical background to the programme and the legislative framework has been examined by a range of authors (Eddy, 1991; Hadorn, 1991; Dixon and Welch, 1991) and will not be rehearsed here. The relevant issue for our discussion lies in the characterization of Oregon as a 'social utility' or 'reasonableness' model: impact on public health, costs and effectiveness of treatments, number of cases, social costs of treating versus not treating. This involved the production of league tables through a series of meetings with communities and telephone surveys whereby people were asked to valuate different health states. This was backed up by literature searches, expert advice and public debate about the rankings. After revisions a 'final' ranking was produced which pairs specific conditions with treatments which appear to be effective. The latter contention is the apparent Achilles heel of the programme as evidence about effectiveness remains patchy, and often reflects professional prejudice, rather than robust findings. The rapidly growing literature on effectiveness aims, in time, to assess clinical interventions, but at present acceptance of why effectiveness studies have to be carried out and made public is starting to gain credence. The next step of how these studies should be carried out has only just begun (Riley *et al.*, 1995).

According to Maynard (1994) and other critics, the Oregon listing relies too much on guesses, and therefore no firm foundation exists for making choices about the balance between costs and presumed health gain. Daniels (1991) raises another issue which is important for our discussion about community involvement in priority-setting. He argues that while the generation of values concerned the Medicaid recipients (that is, the poor uninsured people), those who were involved in making those choices were disproportionately drawn from groups such as health professionals, the white, the educated and the well-off. Thus, the community involved was unrepresentative of the target community, or as Daniels put it more forcefully 'the "haves" deciding what is "important" to give the "have-nots"' (p.2234). While representation can be conceived of in various ways – as discussed in Chapter 3 – it is important to be transparent and rigorous about the sample selection in order to produce credible results. The criticism of the method for community involvement in Oregon is both technically justified, but more importantly, points to the difficulty of adequately representing the experience of health and illness, which requires a careful selection of people who are able to reflect the subjectivity and values embedded in that experience.

Moving away from the specific Oregon example, a number of related issues have emerged from research carried out in Britain and two examples are relevant within this context. The first study by Bowling and colleagues (1993) aimed to explore the values of a deprived inner London community in relation to health services, to assess the representativeness of these views and to compare the public's choices with those of professionals such as hospital consultants, GPs and public health physicians. Co-operation from community groups was secured and intensive group discussions and questionnaires were the main devices in obtaining their views. A further survey was administered to a random sample from the general population. The three groups of doctors were surveyed by postal questionnaire. The findings of this study replicated the order of priorities reported in other studies: life saving treatment as the highest priority, care for people with chronic and mental health problems as middle or low priority, and health education and family planning as low priority (Crawshaw *et al.*, 1990). The researchers provide a caveat that the community does not, of course, present a homogenous view and that differences in prioritization emerged in relation to age and health status, this will be highlighted in the next study. Priorities assigned by the doctors differed from those of the community, but also differed between the three professional groupings, reflecting their specific concerns. For example, doctors ranked mental illness as a high priority while the community ranked it as a middle to low priority; health education was ranked high by public health doctors while GPs and consultants ranked it towards the lower end of the scale.

The key issues raised by this study were that community involvement in priority-setting is complex, and methodologies are still evolving. However, Bowling and colleagues argue that face-to-face interviews with a random sample of the population are essential in achieving representative views. Of course, this does not mean that the community values are 'right'. Providing clear and objective information can assist the community in their ability to weigh up evidence, and the methodological tool kit has to be further refined to ascertain the variety and depth of views necessary. On these last two points the study has attracted criticism (Pfeffer and Pollock, 1993a, 1993b): first, information about effectiveness and cost-effectiveness of many interventions, as stated before, remains incomplete. Furthermore, it is important that a distinction be drawn between asking communities about their values (like in the Oregon exercise) or asking them directly about priority-setting. For the latter purpose complete information has to be distributed, and people have to be made aware of the responsibility they take on, as their opinion may lead to the denial of certain types of care. It is difficult to ascertain from a value-based ranking whether people actually feel that specific services should be withdrawn. Second, surveys do not provide an understanding of the context within which people make choices, that is, the influence of the political and socio-cultural environment, and these aspects crucially determine people's judgements. Thus, methodological refinements should be in the area of exploring the process of forming opinions and preferences, alongside validation in larger-scale samples.

The second UK example reiterates and elaborates upon the above-mentioned issues. Hopton and Dlugolecka (1995) aimed to assess the feasibility of using patients' perceptions of need for primary health care services in order to formulate priorities. They build on the growing body of research which has expressed concern about representativeness of community views, including minority subgroups, and the depth and breadth of knowledge that the public has about services, in particular concerning alternative provisions. Methodological difficulty exists when distinguishing between general or personal preferences, and conceptual problems arise around the definition of perceived need versus popularity. Hopton and Dlugolecka attempt to remedy some of these issues in their study. They began by designing a questionnaire in collaboration with primary care professionals covering areas of primary health and social care. The questionnaire asked respondents which services would be currently of great (some or no) help to them personally. The questionnaire, together with a health status questionnaire (the SF-36, Brazier *et al.*, 1992) was distributed to a stratified random sample of general practice populations in Lothian.

Using a health status measure alongside the preferences questionnaire, and by limiting the scope to primary health and social care services, some of the criticisms of earlier studies could be resolved. Most importantly, differences between healthy and unhealthy respondents could be clearly defined, and the authors argue that the assessment of need based on general populations differs from an assessment of need based on ill-health. Thus, the distinction can be made between perceived need and so-called popularity. For example, less healthy people report more services as being helpful, and coping with pain and stress figure prominently. Similarities between healthy and unhealthy subgroups exist and this was notable with regard to the top priority of regular health checks. In comparison with the Bowling *et al.* study, Hopton and Dlugolecka demonstrate quite different priorities because they have narrowed down the field by taking out the secondary and tertiary care interventions, thus avoiding the danger of over-representation of heroic interventions. This approach provides a more precise delineation of preferences, and services which deal with pain management and welfare benefits receive high rankings.

The study raised important questions about equality and equity: while everybody has an equal chance of expressing their preferences, this could contradict the principle of equity, where minority needs could be severe, but remain under-represented. Solutions have to be found to address the balance between equality and equity, and integrating more formal measurements such as QALYs within the process could compare need and health gain within a broader framework of comprehensive community involvement. The second issue reinforces a point made earlier, namely whether communities fully understand the purpose of priority-setting research and its implications. Information alone may not be sufficient, but the involvement of people throughout the total process of needs assessment, priority-setting, implementation and evaluation might begin to provide them with a robust knowledge base for decision-making. This also means, that instead of Hopton and Dlugolecka's method of asking professionals to draw up the questionnaire, communities should be involved in the design of research tools and thus share control over all stages of the policy process.

The approach adopted in the Netherlands for defining a basic package of health care does not primarily represent research-based priority-setting, but a philosophical framework which provides a guide to making choices. Like the Oregon model it is a step-wise process: first, prioritizing diagnosis/treatment pairs in priority order on the basis of value to the community, value to the potential patient, and the need to be included in the basic package; second, ordering the diagnosis/treatment pairs according to their net added value; third, weighing the results, using a number of 'reasonable' criteria (Dunning, 1992, p.84). Through the system of criteria the Dunning Committee tried to formulate a coherent framework, integrating the assessment with the notion of solidarity. Solidarity is defined as risk solidarity, when the healthy pay for the sick, and income solidarity, when the wealthy pay for the poor and good risks pay for the bad risks. This means that there will be population-wide solidarity allowing risks to be more equally distributed, but at the same time a measure of individual responsibility will remain. The four criteria are the following:

1. Necessary care: services which can be useful to all members of the general population, and which guarantees their normal function as a member of the community, or simply protect their existence; services aimed at maintaining or restoring ability to participate in social life; services which serve to prevent serious injury to health in the long term; services where need is determined by the severity of the disease, and by the number of sufferers.
2. Effectiveness: only care for which the effectiveness has been confirmed and documented can be included in the basic package.
3. Efficiency: using cost-effectiveness and cost-utility analyses, limits should be set for efficiency below which services should be excluded.
4. Individual responsibility: certain services should be left to individuals to select, especially when costs are high and effects limited.

The main criticism levelled at the framework is its lack of precision, such as the vague manner in which individual responsibility is defined, and its lack of realism, in particular concerning effectiveness. Maynard (1994) argues that if this criterion was to be applied properly the cost of health care everywhere would be cut magnificently (p.6). Conversely, the Dutch model proposes a more integrated, philosophical approach based on public debate and social consensus, to setting priorities.

Comparing the methods for priority-setting discussed so far, a number of concerns which Green and Barker (1988) raised remain to be addressed. The formal measurements such as the QALY rely explicitly on the belief that priority-setting can be done as a rational and objective process. Oregon and the Netherlands acknowledge the more subjective input of communities, but assess their preferences against expert judgements, which could be implicitly biased towards the preservation of particular professional interests. As such, the community preferences are receiving less weight than the expert ones. The two specific examples from Britain attempt to overcome this duality by placing expert and lay perspectives alongside each other. However, they do not confront the question of rationality, that is, whether the preferences that communities express fit and can be analysed within a scientific, rational framework. Little attention is paid to the way in which people arrive at decisions, the temporal structure of choices and the influences of psychological, social and cultural circumstances cannot be taken into account within the adopted survey approach.

The other point highlighted by Green and Barker is that priority-setting exercises rarely deal with the reallocation of existing resources. Ostensibly preferred values are being sought across the full range of services, but when actually examining implementation, changes tend to be made in the allocation of new resources and do not include disinvestment decisions. In the British context this is borne out when scrutinizing purchasing plans of health authorities, who are charged with changing service configurations in line with needs and preferences of local populations. Klein and Redmayne (1992) reported in their survey of 114 health authorities that only 12 had moved away from traditional patterns of provision, and had begun to formulate policies about priorities and rationing.

The brief overview of priority-setting methods emphasizes that the role of the community has to be examined in more detail, and in particular why, who and how communities should be involved. This means that both the structure and process of priority-setting have to be assessed on their capacity to integrate community perspectives.

COMMUNITY PRIORITIES

The question of why communities should be involved in determining health policy, of which priority-setting is an integral part, has already been addressed in Chapter 3. However, it is important to rehearse the argument here from a slightly different vantage point. Involving communities in decision-making appears to be an essential element in a democratic approach to policy making, and certainly is considered as one of the cornerstones of the WHO Primary Health Care approach. Public participation can be seen as counterbalancing the otherwise unopposed and implicit expert decisions on priority-setting. However, Donovan and Coast (1994) pose the important question as to whether the public could and should be forced to make unpalatable judgements. They argue that priority-setting involves a series of difficult choices, some of which could be deemed controversial or impossible, such as between life-saving treatment for one young person, versus rehabilitation for old people or support for drug addicts versus treatment for people with kidney failure. These ethical dilemmas of preserving life, caring for young and dependent people, as opposed to looking after so-called undeserving people or the economically inactive, cannot be off-loaded to communities under the banner of democratic participation. Donovan and Coast go on to say that it is doubtful whether the public accepts that experts and decision-makers abrogate their professional responsibility, namely their role of making informed judgements on behalf of the public. Thus, the truth must lie somewhere in between, with community involvement being taken seriously, which implies the creation of proper structures, processes and methods and decision-makers offering their expertise within an open arena of debate.

A number of further issues can then be raised, including opening up the value basis of many professional judgements, and the exercise of prioritization as a social rather than rational scientific process. Weighing up professional, expert advice against community views becomes a rather different proposition, and new ways of assessing evidence have to be created. We have already discussed the difficulty of deciding who the community is and therefore, whose preferences are being tapped. Here, we are concerned with the question of how we place different perspectives alongside each other, each representing different world views and experiences of social (and health) reality. The method discussed above (Bowling *et al.*, 1993) attempted to compare professional and public preferences, but did not question the basis on which the various groupings arrived at their preferred options. This is not intended as a criticism, rather to point out the difficulty of aggregating individual preferences into a composite one which represents a credible social preference. Donovan and Coast argue (following the principle of Arrow's Impossibility Theorem) that there is no perfect way of making social choices through aggregating individual preferences.

While it may be impossible to find a perfect method, it is possible to examine the way decisions are arrived at, and assess the contribution of communities in the decision-making process. McKeown and colleagues put the question as follows: purchasers (of health care) should 'concentrate on the *quality* of their priority-setting processes rather than the *"scientific correctness"* of their final decisions on priorities' (original emphasis) (p.21). They go on to state that the priority-setting process should be transparent and therefore has to reflect the contradictions, confusions and conflicts which priority-setting inevitably engenders. This approach explicitly acknowledges that priority-setting is not a rational, incremental measurement process, but is a social, value-based activity which, as a result, has to explore the different perspectives underlying the expressed preferences.

The acceptance of the notion that priority-setting is value-based has implications for the way in which decision-making is structured. In many health systems priority-setting continues to be conceived as a rational, technical process whereby the involvement of communities is approached in a manner consistent with rationality. Often, public preferences are ascertained through the use of surveys or specific market research approaches such as focus groups. Generally, the quantitative measurement of public opinion is considered as the accepted scientific method. Increasingly, this is being questioned as the best approach of listening to users, and in particular, tapping the views of those who are traditionally not heard. Alternative methods, mainly drawn from the qualitative research tradition, have been advocated as appropriate to understanding people's views and preferences related to the context in which they experience health and illness (Sykes *et al.*, 1992). It can be argued that too much attention is focused on the methodological aspects of how to gain public preferences, and treating it as a technical issue, rather than looking at whether the structures and processes are actually conducive to involving communities.

The structural question poses uncomfortable problems about power, and the dominance of particular world views (and we have addressed this in Chapter 4). Focusing, in particular, on the structure of decision-making in priority-setting a range of uncertainties arise: professionals such as Public Health doctors and medical specialists, health economists or managers are cast in the role of experts who make decisions on the basis of evidence. The reality is that there is little or uneven scientific evidence on effectiveness and cost-effectiveness, which makes the structural position of the decision-makers less secure. Instead, the implicit social (and sometimes political) judgements that are at play need to be laid bare, so that both the structure and process of decision-making can be extended to become a more equal participation of experts and so-called non-experts. If priority-setting is acknowledged to be a social process, using scientific evidence as and when possible, then the involvement of communities is no longer a question of seeking or granting their opinions. Instead, community views are considered as an equally important contribution to making choices, and responsibility for the outcomes of the priority-setting process can be shared more evenly. Thus, it does not absolve professionals from making difficult decisions, nor does it overload communities with problems they cannot resolve. Rather, the different types of expertise can be brought into play, in order to weigh up the 'hard' evidence against the more 'experiential' evidence, and conflicts, ambiguities or uncertainties have to be confronted in the process.

Within this process it remains important to clarify the methods used to accumulate evidence, the values on which choices are based, and in view of incomplete knowledge assumptions have to be made explicit. The transparency of the process, and thus the improved accountability of those involved, should improve the quality of the process. The learning experience is double-sided: decision-makers learn to assess experience-based data and to understand the impact of policy decisions on people's real lives; communities learn to understand and evaluate scientific data and how to base decisions on this body of information. Ultimately, priority-setting is a process that involves conflict and contradictions, and often will not arrive at a 'happy ending', but as McKeown and colleagues insist, the quality of the process and the methodology used are important. As an extension of this point it could be argued that if the process is good, it can form a solid foundation for a sustainable relationship between communities and decision-makers, and, in the long term, offer real benefits in terms of commitment to the priorities set, and the making of a commonly owned health policy.

Priority-setting in Rapid Appraisal

One of the key objectives of Rapid Appraisal is to determine priority needs of a community. The steps outlined in the Rapid Appraisal process are first, to define community concerns through a series of qualitative interviews, and comparison with other data sets (which will be discussed in the next chapter), and second, on the basis of these concerns engage in a priority-setting exercise. The priority-setting methods are not set in stone, but are variations on a central theme, namely that the priorities as chosen by the community are of equal value to those chosen by professionals and managers. The way in which this comparison can be drawn is determined locally, and can take the form of, for example, a statistical comparison, or a weighted approach. In some Rapid Appraisals a further distinction is drawn between professionals who reside in the community, such as for example, the vicar, and professionals who live outside the community.

If a statistical comparison is chosen, the first step is to collate individual preferences on the derived list of community concerns. The choice is then between different statistical tools. The two tools chosen in most Rapid Appraisals are the following:

- The Kendall's coefficient of concordance which examines the level of agreement within each of the sets of 'judges', i.e. any individual invited to participate in the priority-setting. They have to rank order the priorities in each of the categories of the Rapid Appraisal information profile. The scores are compared with each other within each category, and the lowest score denotes the highest priority. Significance values ($p<0.001$; $p<0.01$ and $p<0.05$) range from high to lower levels. Thus, when the p-value is <0.001 the level of agreement between the judges is great.

- The Kruskal–Wallis one-way ANOVA explains whether and how the ranking of priorities differ significantly between sets of judges. A p-value of <0.001 means that there is a high degree of difference between the judges. Thus, in the case of the example below, the community displayed diverging views on the issue of education, even though it came up as the second highest priority.

(For detailed statistical guidance reference should be made to specialist statistics books such as Siegel and Castellan, 1988).

The following examples demonstrate the use of these statistical measures. The first example is from Bridgemere, where the distinction is drawn between the Rapid Appraisal professional team's preferences, and those expressed by the community. The latter can be divided into the 'informal' community, namely the people who live in the community, and the 'formal' community, people who work and live in the community.

Table 5.1 Priority listing from Bridgemere

	Staff	*Community*	
	(n = 9)	*(n = 19)*	*(n = 15)*
Community capacity			
Apathy	1.7**	1.8***	1.3***
No community centre	1.8	2.3	2.5
Prejudice towards outsiders	3.7	3.7	3.2
Single parents	2.9	2.2	3.0 +
The Community's own valuable resources			
Good informal information networks	1.7***	2.0	2.1
Community spirit	2.9	2.3	2.1 +
Supportive family networks	1.4	1.7	1.9
Socio-economic environment			
Unemployment	2.0	1.7**	1.7*
Poverty and deprivation	2.7	2.9	2.9
Poor education	3.0	3.1	3.1
Disease and disability			
Smoking and drinking	2.1***	3.1	3.2*
Acceptance of ill health	3.2	3.7	3.5
Hard drugs	5.8	4.7	5.1
Chronic illness	5.9	4.6	3.7 +
Respiratory disease	3.7	3.2	3.1
Poor diet	3.2	4.3	4.1
Inadequate parenting skills	4.1	4.1	5.1
Health, social, environmental services			
Services inadequate	2.4**	2.9***	2.4
Poor information on aids/adaptations	4.4	4.2	3.5
No GP or chemist on the estate	2.8	3.2	3.6
Disabled facilities poor	3.4	2.7	2.4
Teenagers, nothing to do	1.9	1.9	3.2 +
Physical environment			
Pollution	5.4***	4.4	3.7**
Security	2.1	2.6	2.6
Dogs	4.9	4.4	5.0
Rats and rubbish	5.9	4.5	4.1 +
Dangerous roads	3.7	4.5	5.3

Inadequate housing and allocation	2.8	3.7	4.1	
Little open space	3.2	3.9	3.1	

Notes: *Agreement* (Kendall's coefficient of concordance) significant within judges for each 'block' of planning profile: ***, $p < 0.001$; **, $p < 0.01$; *, $p < 0.05$. Ranking of priorities significantly different (Kruskal–Wallis one-way ANOVA) between sets of judges: +, $p < 0.05$.

The community and professionals both had apathy at the top of the list of community resource problems, while at the same time supportive family networks were considered to be an asset. There was also agreement on the socio-economic problems, with unemployment being the top priority. The community considered respiratory illness the main issue, but they were very close in their judgement to the professionals who saw smoking and drinking as the key problem. Professionals felt that the fact that there were no activities for teenagers was most important, while the community placed services and disabled facilities at the top. Finally security was seen by everyone as a prime issue to be tackled.

The second example is from Sandown, where a further refinement is introduced, namely a distinction between the Rapid Appraisal team's preferences based on their professional perspective, and the preferences they perceive as being the ones from the community itself (that is, the team members judge priorities as if they are the community).

Table 5.2 Priority listing from Sandown

	Staff		Community		
	Self (n = 9)	*Community* (n = 9)	*Formal* (n = 24)	*Informal* (n = 8)	
Priorities: *listed under each planning profile category*					
Socio-economic					
Unemployment	2.0**	1.3***	2.4***	3.0**	
Poverty	3.0	2.4	3.4	4.4	
No prospects for young people	3.7	3.0	3.3	4.4	
Lack of parental control	4.1	4.6	3.5	2.0	+
Negative view of education	4.7	6.8	4.1	2.9	+++
Teenage pregnancy	5.1	4.8	5.6	5.8	
Organized bullying	5.4	5.1	5.8	5.6	
Disease and disability					
Smoking	2.2	4.4*	2.6***	3.5	
Poverty as health hazard	3.3	3.0	3.1	4.1	
Young children's health	3.8	3.1	3.7	4.4	
Asthma and respiratory disease	4.2	4.0	4.2	3.3	

Alcohol	4.7	5.3	3.7	3.9	
Drug use	4.8	2.6	4.7	4.3	+
Risky sexual behaviour	5.0	5.6	5.8	4.6	
Health and environmental services					
Conflicting advice between health professionals	2.2	3.4*	2.0	2.3	+
Lack of facilities at health centre	2.4	1.7	2.3	3.5	+
Health services and staff off-putting	2.6	2.2	2.9	2.3	
GPs are not responsive	2.8	2.7	2.8	2.0	
Social services					
Only available in a crisis	2.2	2.7	2.1*	2.3	
Lack of information	2.2	3.0	2.3	2.1	
Long waiting times for services	2.6	2.2	2.9	2.3	
Threat of taking children away	3.0	1.6	2.3	3.5	++
Physical environment					
Feeling unsafe	2.3	3.2***	2.0**	2.9**	
Vandalism	2.4	2.4	2.8	1.9	
Lack of policing	3.0	2.3	3.3	2.9	
Speeding cars/joyriding	3.4	2.1	3.9	2.6	
Lack of housing choice	3.8	4.9	3.7	4.8	+

Notes: *Agreement* (Kendall's coefficient of concordance) significant within judges for each 'block' of planning profile: ***, $p < 0.001$; **, $p < 0.01$; *, $p < 0.05$. Ranking of priorities significantly different (Kruskal–Wallis one-way ANOVA) between sets of judges: +++, $p < 0.001$; ++, $p < 0.01$; +, $p < 0.05$.

This example demonstrates the differences between the community perspectives and the professionals, with for example lack of parental control, asthma and respiratory disease, unresponsive GPs, lack of information on social services, and vandalism being the community priorities; while the professionals thought the community would put first: unemployment, drug use, lack of facilities in the health centre, social services' threat of taking children away, and speeding cars. These differences have then to be debated in order to move forward to the next phase of action planning.

A weighted approach was taken in Woodforde where a simple method was adopted: the issue given the highest rank within a category by each judge was given the maximum number of points within that category. For example, if six issues were mentioned within the category, priority one attracted six points, while priority six attracted one point. The scores were then summed across all judges (community and Rapid Appraisal team together) and the issue with the highest number of points became the top priority. Results are given in the following Table 5.3.

Table 5.3 Priority listing from Woodforde

Issue	Score	Rank order
Provision of more leisure facilities, including swimming pool	28	1
A focal point is needed for the community	26	2
More information about Social Services	20	3
Nothing to do for young people	18	4
Local Authority must listen to community	15	5 (joint)
Councillors must have higher local profile	15	5 (joint)
Lack of public transport, especially for elderly people	13	6 (joint)
Drainage problems	13	6 (joint)
Prevention of under-age drinking	9	7

The priority listings are derived from a direct comparison of professional and community preferences, and thus do not provide insight into the value judgements on which choices are based. This is an apparent weakness of the Rapid Appraisal methodology, and it is important to consider possible options to remedy this lack of context. In terms of community perspectives, the value basis can, to a limited extent, be derived from the in-depth interviews which are carried out with key respondents in order to develop the issues listings. However, they only offer insight into how people arrive at a range of priorities, but not how they select between priorities, and the reasons behind the preferences. The theoretical problem of whether choices are made on the basis of popularity, actual need, perceptions of effectiveness and so on, remains unanswered. One option is to discuss the final priority listing with the people who have been involved in setting those priorities, and asking them to spell out the rationale behind their decisions. When we discuss the feedback loop and sustainability of the Rapid Appraisal we will return to this issue. Continuing dialogue with the community can partly overcome this difficulty through constant re-evaluation of priorities.

The second problem within the Rapid Appraisal lies in how priorities are reformulated in scientific frameworks by using statistical calculations, weighting systems or other similar approaches. By employing these methods, there is an implicit acceptance of the rational approach to priority-setting, and the fundamental social nature of the process is obscured. Conversely, one can argue that the ostensibly rational approach only serves as a point of reference for an open debate with communities about the meaning of the priorities, and the implications of acting on them. If vigilance is observed about the way in which the calculated results are used in formulating local policy, and contextual considerations are taken into account, the scoring of priorities can be interpreted within a relativist framework, that is, accepting that different groupings will view priorities differently, depending on their experience, their sense of power and control and their expectations of effective outcomes.

Data collection and analysis | 6

Rapid Appraisal claims to be based upon a multi-method research design, consistent with the understanding of health as a holistic, multi-faceted experience. As a result, no single methodological tool is able to capture this complex notion of health, and as a corollary, of needs and priorities. A further claim is its flexibility and the possible adoption of a range of methodologies, including innovative cross-disciplinary approaches, if they appear to be locally relevant. This is most noticeable in the applications in the developing world where disease ranking (Welbourn, 1992), body mapping (Cornwall, 1992), 3D (three-dimensional) modelling of neighbourhoods (Gibson, 1994) and so on have been used. The work on which this book is based has taken place within the developed world, and therefore, the methods discussed here are those that appear most applicable to that context. This, of course, does not mean that methods cannot be transposed from one setting to the other, but first-hand experience of applying specific methods can only be claimed from developed countries. For detailed discussion and examples pertaining to developing countries we have to refer to Kumar (1994) and the articles in the series Rapid Rural Appraisal Notes – renamed in 1995 to Notes on Participatory Learning and Action – published by the International Institute for Environment and Development, London.

This chapter discusses the data required to fulfil the dual purpose of a Rapid Appraisal exercise, namely to first formulate a community needs list and second, to derive a priority list from the needs listing. Reference will be made to Chapter 2 and the discussion on needs, and Chapter 5 where priority-setting has been explored. The methodological implications are then discussed, before the theoretical and operational issues concerning the collection and analysis of data are presented. The question of triangulation will be treated separately, and a number of alternative methods concerning priority-setting will be investigated.

COLLECTING DATA ON COMMUNITY NEEDS

We have argued in Chapter 2 that a new methodology for the assessment of needs has to go beyond the epidemiological approach in order to encompass the experience of ill-health. There are several strands to a complex needs assessment, but the purpose of Rapid Appraisal is not to produce a detailed and comprehensive overview of community needs, but rather to use a needs assessment as a starting point for action. A full needs assessment, therefore, is reduced to a number of salient issues on which joint action can be taken between stakeholders from the community and organizations. Consequently, a balance has to be found between a scientifically-based needs assessment, and a practical tool geared to producing outcomes within a limited time frame. This means that a compromise has to be found between a methodological approach, and a focused production of a needs list which can be defended as being based on sound evidence. As a result, we will have to start the discussion with a consideration of methodological principles, and then assess the manner in which Rapid Appraisal can 'trade down' to a quicker and more simple design (Hakim, 1987).

There are many classifications of social research, and of the subsets within it, but they can be roughly distinguished from each other as qualitative and quantitative research, with the former concerned with measurement, and the latter with explanation (Lilford and Harrison, 1994). Both academic researchers and those operating in the area of applied research have increasingly come to realize that this distinction is more of a hindrance than a help, and instead have explored relationships between the two (Brewer and Hunter, 1989; Brannen, 1992; Ong, 1993). Recently, Miles and Huberman (1994) have contributed to this discussion when examining the main approaches to qualitative research, and linkages across to quantitative approaches. They present three main theoretical strands to qualitative data analysis: interpretivism, social anthropology and collaborative social research. For the purpose of this discussion we will selectively focus on specific theoretical and methodological perspectives, such as the latter, where research and action take place within a real social setting. One of the typical methodological stances in this type of research is dialectical, whereby researchers and local actors may have opposing interpretations of the data. Through dialogue and constant feedback, data is processed, and the relationship between researcher and researched tends to become collaborative and one based on equality.

Going on to discuss the relationships between qualitative and quantitative research, Miles and Huberman draw on a range of authors and make the point that while the methods are not always interchangeable, they can strengthen each other's intrinsic qualities. More specifically, they suggest (following Rossman and Wilson, 1984, 1991) that qualitative and quantitative data should be linked because they enable confirmation or corroboration of each other through triangulation (which will be explained below); the analysis can be developed or elaborated through richer data; new lines of thinking can emerge through surprises and paradoxes emanating from comparison of data sets. They go on to discuss the way in which the qualitative and quantitative approaches mutually influence each other at every stage of the research process:

- Design: the quantitative approach helps in finding representative samples and locating deviant cases; the qualitative one assists in conceptual development.
- Data collection: quantitative data serve to provide a background and access information that is often overlooked; the qualitative perspective helps to make access easier and provide an organizing framework for data collection.
- Analysis: quantitative data demonstrate the generality of specific observations, verify or throw new light on qualitative data; qualitative data help to deepen understanding of quantitative findings through interpretation, validation, theorizing.

In order to capitalize on the complementarity of methods, researchers must have a grasp of the key design issues concerning the appropriateness of the choice of method to the research question, whether the link between qualitative and quantitative approaches should be made within the particular design, and if so, how the linkages are being created and exploited.

The above methodological considerations are important in Rapid Appraisal for it combines a range of research methods within its overall design; even though the methods have to be selected according to local circumstances, the broad considerations concerning the qualitative–quantitative continuum have to be taken into account. In concrete terms, therefore, Rapid Appraisal must reconcile a diverse range of data sets, including epidemiological and secondary material on the one hand and biographical accounts on the one other, and different analytical frameworks, most notably one based upon a dialogue with communities. In order to clarify the key methodological issues we will examine each of them in turn.

SECONDARY DATA

In terms of health and social needs, epidemiological data provide an important source of information. Stevens and Raftery (1994) state that, particularly in relation to service planning – which is part of a Rapid Appraisal, prevalence and incidence of disease form key foundations for needs assessment. However, prevalence and incidence are not synonymous with need, and Stevens and Raftery cite the example of the common cold, which although highly prevalent at certain times of the year, does not constitute a great need for services as it is mostly self-limiting. Furthermore, they argue that the availability and quality of data is uneven, and often not suitable for translation into service needs, let alone need more generally. Despite these reservations, epidemiological data and census data continue to offer rich sources of background information. For a Rapid Appraisal the following community-based data are desirable:

- age-sex structure, marital status, social class, ethnic groupings;
- economic activity;
- education and literacy;
- tenure and amenities, car availability, persons per room;
- household composition;
- long-term limiting illness, specific disease and disability categories;
- activity data on acute, primary, community care services.

While Rapid Appraisals are intended to be carried out in relatively homogeneous communities, the secondary data can provide insights into internal differences as the example from Rosehill and Pipegate, two neighbourhoods which are located adjacent to each other, illustrates (Table 6.1).

Table 6.1 Census data (selected) from Rosehill and Pipegate

Economic activity	Rosehill		Pipegate	
	Male	*Female*	*Male*	*Female*
Economically active	1312 (67)	988 (46)	1031 (64)	782 (43)
Economically inactive				
students	91 (5)	104 (6)	44 (3)	51 (3)
permanently sick	131 (7)	95 (4)	183 (11)	95 (5)
retired	391 (20)	451 (21)	325 (20)	419 (23)
Other inactive	18 (1)	499 (23)	12 (1)	472 (26)
Total aged 16 and over	1943	2137	1595	1819

Percentages are given in parentheses.

The differences between the two communities are small with a somewhat higher level of economic activity in Rosehill than in Pipegate, and higher level of male permanent sickness in Pipegate. Using the traditional social class structure indicators, Rosehill has a predominance of social class I and II at 58%, while Pipegate has a preponderance of class III at 53%. In Rosehill, 27% of households report that a member suffers from long-standing limiting illness, while the figure in Pipegate is 35%. Taken these, and other indicators, together it seems that health and social status is higher in Rosehill than in Pipegate, and this offers a first level overview of comparative issues to be pursued in the Rapid Appraisal.

In Britain, Directors of Public Health produce their annual report on the health of the local populations (which vary in size from 250 000 to over 1 million people) based upon census indicators, mortality and morbidity data and service usage. This material can often be disaggregated to the level of localities and communities reporting small area statistics as given in Table 6.1. Alongside this report, Local Authorities produce their Community Care Plans, which offer quantitative data on, for example, physical disability, child protection and the well-being of the elderly population. These types of reports provide insight into expressed need (demand) and availability of services. Stevens and Raftery (1994) are, however, cautious about the usefulness of these type of data sources, because often service components, and their relationship to need, are not clearly defined. Furthermore, process rather than outcome data is collected and therefore appropriateness and effectiveness of services cannot be determined with accuracy. Two additional complicating factors are that: first, services cover a continuum of care, from prevention, intervention or treatment to rehabilitation and discharge; and second, people vary in terms of severity of disease, or urgency of problems. Both factors determine the needs framework, but little systematic knowledge exists allowing the interaction between need and services to operate at a sophisticated level. This general problem affects the more local use of this type of data in Rapid Appraisals. One alternative option is to move beyond local material, and set it within a broader context of national (or international) data. In reality, evidence on effectiveness and cost-effectiveness cannot be collated reliably at a small scale; therefore, comparisons offer valuable insights into the representativeness or peculiarity of the local situation. For example, a number of Rapid Appraisals have pointed to difficulties in accessing information on Social Services and the limited availability of very specific skills and resources. This is a broader problem, related directly to cost-containment policies of Local Authorities and the more stringent use of accessibility criteria. While this finding does not invalidate the local experience, the wider context explains that the problem exists at the level of policy rather than that it depends on local targeting. Consequently, solutions to this problem have to be formulated at the appropriate level and therefore do not result in wasted local effort and disillusionment.

More informal secondary data are useful for a Rapid Appraisal. The examples are legion, but could include *ad hoc* reports by voluntary organizations about specific problems or services; for example, the problems of ethnic minorities or drug users. Individual professionals often write papers with a particular purpose, for example, Health Visitors construct health profiles of neighbourhoods, which contain locally relevant information. Qualitative secondary data includes diaries, life histories, photographic records, tape recordings and so on. Most of this material is not 'purpose-built' for assessing health and social needs, but provides indirect guidance. The analysis of this type of material poses its own methodological challenges, because the implicit meanings of its authors have to be uncovered or presumed. The researchers have to draw up explicit criteria by which this material can be evaluated, and we will address this issue when discussing data analysis in Rapid Appraisal.

OBSERVATION

In many developed countries the emphasis in data collection tends to be on the written word and the validity of this material often depends on its representation as intelligible rational accounts. The value of other types of material have been underestimated, in particular by quantitative social scientists. Conversely, anthropologists, like archaeologists, have emphasized the importance of material culture and studied the symbolic value of the environment (man-made and natural) and artefacts. Rapid Appraisals carried out in the developing world have tended to pay more attention to these aspects of human living than those done in the developed world, and mapping exercises are an important example of this focus (Colombani *et al.*, 1992).

When carrying out observations, people *and* their environment are both important subjects for research. Most research literature has described participant observation, while pure observation has been relatively neglected (Adler and Adler, 1994). Pure observation is located at the other end of the spectrum as opposed to complete membership in naturalistic settings, with gradations of participation in between. Whatever form of observation is being practised the observers tend to draw on their own cultural knowledge or what can be termed common sense, which implicitly contains culturally informed interpretations of what is seen. The danger of bias is particularly great if observation is carried out by one person, or when no cross-checking with interview or other data is available. Within the Rapid Appraisal exercise, observation serves to augment other data sets, and is carried out by groups of observers. Thus validity of observational material is less of a problem through triangulation and inter-observer comparison. Furthermore, observation in Rapid Appraisal tends to focus less on human interaction patterns, but pays most attention to environmental factors and the way people shape and interpret the environment. This places boundaries upon the locus of observation, and defines the parameters within which observers operate.

Given those clear delineations the observation process has to follow clearly agreed stages and conform to agreed criteria. While the observation does not have to correspond to the same rigorous rules of in-depth social science research certain methodologies can be adopted. Focused observations can be guided by notational records, defining a specific range of observation categories, and in the case of Rapid Appraisal these include features of the physical environment, structure and use of the environment, artefacts, impact of the

Table 6.2 Recording framework for Rosehill and Pipegate: road safety (1995, illustrative only)

Location	Traffic density	Traffic lights	Pedestrian crossings	Cycle paths	Pavement width	Play space	Street lighting
High Street	Very busy, narrow lanes, no bus lane	At key crossing	At key crossing, not in front of shops	None	Narrow pavement in front of busy shops	None	Good
Dog Lane	Busy, narrow and main through road	At two main inter-sections	At traffic lights only	None	Narrow, apart in front of terraced houses	None	Adequate
Beam Street	Busy dual carriage way (no bus route)	At key crossing	At traffic lights and in middle	Cycle path throughout	Wide pavements throughout	Small green area at top of road	Good
Church Lane	Quiet, no bus route	None	None	None	Sufficient width	Play area in park	Adequate

etc.

Table 6.3 Recording framework for Rosehill and Pipegate

Location	Terraced	Semi-detached	Detached	General state of repair	Specific problems	Cleanliness
High Street	All houses, 30% used as shops			50% in poor state	Mainly structural problems	Dirty front gardens and pavements
Dog Lane	40% (appear to be used as flats)	60%		Terraced houses in poor state	Mainly structural problems	Reasonably clean private spaces
Beam Street		70%	30%	Good state of repair	Few minor problems	Clean private and public spaces
Church Lane	80%	20%		Reasonable state of repair	Mainly roof problems in terraces	Reasonable cleanliness overall

etc.

environment on behaviours and so on. Examples of recording sheets are given in Tables 6.2 and 6.3.

In relation to validity the importance of cross-checking between observers has already been mentioned. Adler and Adler (1994) offer a further test of validity whereby the observers use a style of writing which closely reflects the experiences of the subjects. This can then be validated by the community itself as being authentic to their interpretation of their world. This has particular relevance within Rapid Appraisal by giving communities control over the data gathering process through assessing its authenticity (Atkinson, 1990).

A final problem mentioned by Adler and Adler (1994) is reliability in terms of time and place. Again, within Rapid Appraisal observations are carried out at different times, across different locations in the community, and by different observers. This offers the opportunity to draw multiple comparisons across the observational data in order to maximize reliability. Especially in combination with other data-collection methods, observation becomes a powerful tool in validating research material because it fully exploits researchers' own knowledge and theoretical judgement as guidance to the interpretation of data.

INTERVIEWING

Interviewing is a social science research method par excellence, because it assists in finding out about people and their everyday life and behaviour. In fact, authors have argued that verbal data constitute the cornerstone of social research, but despite this status there has been much less debate about the theoretical interpretation of why questioning affords privileged insights. Foddy (1993) reviews the literature on the interview method and highlights a number of theoretical perspectives: (i) the interview is perceived as social interaction (Phillips, 1971), albeit it a highly specific, and to some extent artificial one; (ii) the interview as a form of communication in which cognitive and linguistic processes play a part (Cicourel, 1982); (iii) the view that interviews cannot be divorced from the social and cultural context of the respondent (Briggs, 1986). Feminist scholars offer an alternative perspective and argue that the interview itself has to change as a tool in social research, and that the fundamental contradiction between the need for 'rapport' between the interviewer and respondent on the one hand, and the collection of reliable and valid data cannot be resolved. Instead, when feminists engage in interviewing they invest their own personal identity in the interview relationship and recognize that 'personal involvement is more than dangerous bias – it is the condition under which people come to know each other and to admit others into their lives' (Oakley, 1981, p.58).

While different theoretical perspectives exist, a common understanding of the interview is that it represents both a conversation and an instrument for data collection. The theoretical perspective, however, crucially determines the way in which an interview is conceived and carried out. For example, the contextual approach to interviewing places emphasis on cultural values and concepts and attempts to arrive at a holistic understanding of the verbal material, alongside other data sources which help in reconstructing the cultural environment. For a feminist researcher a key issue to consider is the shared gender socialization and cultural experience between interviewer and interviewee. This moves the relationship away from the objective, clean research relationship towards one that is 'more complex, messy, various and much more interesting' (Bell and Encel, 1978, p.4). The more technical considerations will, as a result, differ between researchers, ranging from a concern to minimizing interviewer bias to establishing non-hierarchical relationships between interviewer and interviewee. It is beyond the scope of this chapter to engage in these methodological discussions, but we will review a number of interview methods appropriate to the purpose and philosophy of Rapid Appraisal, and discuss technical issues relevant to these methods.

One of the key underlying concerns of Rapid Appraisal is equity, and consequently, specific attention is being paid to the views of people who traditionally would not be able to access policy-makers. Locating the 'natural' methodological home of Rapid Appraisal stems directly from its focus on equity, and can be broadly defined as participatory (or emancipatory) research. Interviewing within this approach is conceived in a way similar to feminist research, whereby the social relationship between interviewer and interviewee should be non-hierarchical, based on reciprocity and genuine dialogue, and where the interpretations of the respondent are considered crucially important. In particular, when researching community's perceptions of needs, the experience of living within the community becomes the focus of attention, and ethnographic (or in-depth, unstructured) interviewing is the main device for exploring subjectivity within an interview, that is a human-to-human relationship (Spradley, 1979).

Most commonly, the strengths of the unstructured interview are said to lie in the greater breadth as it allows the complexity in human thoughts and behaviours to be explored without imposing *a priori* categorization that may limit the field of inquiry (Fontana and Frey, 1994). Foddy (1993) however, critically evaluates some of the established notions about this type of interviewing based upon the use of open questions. First, open questions allow respondents to express themselves in their own words. Foddy argues that following up open questions with so-called probes which clarify the original question, often turns this question into a closed one. Second, answers to open questions indicate the level of the respondent's knowledge about the specific topic. According to Foddy the situation is more complex because people often only respond if they know the answer, want to divulge the information or do not want to look ignorant. Third, it is often assumed that answers to questions indicate what issues are salient to the respondent, but salience can mean a number of things: importance, most easily remembered, being in the forefront of someone's mind at a particular point in time and so on. The same doubts arise around people's strength of feelings.

These issues are important when carrying out unstructured interviews within the Rapid Appraisal, and raise a number of technical and methodological questions. If an interview is to be carried out as a genuine dialogue between people, the agenda will be determined by both parties, and it stops being a straightforward question-and-answer session. Instead, interviewees also ask questions, for example, wanting to know how the interviewer assesses particular needs or priorities. Rather than considering the 'questioning back' as contamination, answering questions as honestly as possible can be considered part of the reciprocal relationship, and the breaking down of the researcher–researched hierarchy. Oakley (1981) stresses that interviewees should be reassured that they are not being exploited by researchers, and within the Rapid Appraisal emphasis should be placed upon the purpose of the interview as eliciting the community's own perspective on need in order to make their voice heard in policy-making. This, of course, requires careful management within the interview situation, and relates to the issue of whether people provide answers that indicate both their knowledge of the topic under discussion, and its salience. Reflecting back in their own words, checking out through repeat questions, getting another member of the interview team to ask the same question, are possible devices for testing this out. The nature of an unstructured interview allows the interviewer to stay close to the interviewee's experience, and this should be maintained throughout.

The above discussion has been based upon the implicit assumption that interviews are based upon an individual being interviewed. Rapid Appraisal also uses group interviews, both in the formulation of the needs list and in the priority-setting exercise. The methods, however, differ in these two stages and will be discussed in turn. For the first stage of generating community concerns the unstructured format is employed. The starting point will be the same as for individual interviews by using open-ended questions, but a group interview also exploits group dynamics whereby the evolving patterns of group interaction provide important research material (Fontana and Frey, 1994). At the same time, the group interview requires skilful handling by the interviewer because an individual or small subgroup can easily dominate discussions, sensitive issues may be suppressed, group pressure to express a 'common' view may prohibit other views to be aired and so on. Many different types of group interviews exist

Table 6.4 Types of group interviews for use in Rapid Appraisal, first stage

Type	Setting	Role of interviewer	Question format	Purpose
Brainstorming	Formal group e.g. professional or informal, e.g. youth club	Non-directive	Unstructured	Exploratory
Field, natural group, e.g. support group for young mothers	Informal spontaneous	(Moderately) non-directive	Unstructured	Exploratory phenomenological (see note)
Field, formal groups, e.g. primary health care team	Preset, but in field	(Somewhat) directive	Semi-structured	Phenomenological

After Fontana and Frey (1994).
For a discussion of phenomenology, see Moustakas (1994). It can be briefly described as an approach which emphasizes subjectivity and the discovery of the essence of experiences. It utilizes only the data available to consciousness, that is the appearance of objects.

views to be aired and so on. Many different types of group interviews exist (Baker, 1991); those relevant for the Rapid Appraisal are shown in Table 6.4

In the second stage of setting priorities, the most useful format for the group interviews is the focus group. This method has been extensively used in market research and can be defined as a carefully planned discussion, designed to obtain perceptions on a defined area of interest in a permissive, non-threatening environment (Krueger, 1994). The planned discussion is focused on a specified problem, has a clear purpose, and as such can be considered highly structured. The group discussions tend to be guided by a moderator who follows a sequence of questions and filters in order to collect data on the perceptions, feelings and ways of thinking of the group members. The focused method appears to be suitable for the second stage as it provides a strong framework for delivering clear outcomes, in this case a list of priorities.

The focus group should consist of people who demonstrate on the one hand homogeneity in terms of shared experiences and social contexts, while on the other hand should not be prejudiced about each others' thoughts and reactions (Stewart and Shamdasani, 1990), which means they should not be familiar with each other. These conditions are important in order to allow exploration of complex perceptions and behaviours, for new ideas to emerge from the group and to stimulate diversity of opinion. In the case of Rapid Appraisal, the focus group approach helps to establish priority-setting as a social rather than rational process, and the various influences upon interpretations of priorities can be discussed through the group process. Using the focus group method alongside individually-based ranking procedures can provide valuable insights into the psychological and socio-cultural reasoning underlying priority-setting.

ANALYSING DATA

Both in quantitative and qualitative social research a large body of knowledge has been produced about the analysis of data. This analysis cannot be divorced from the theoretical framework adopted, and thus, there are a multitude of analytical approaches depending on the purpose of research: measurement, explanation or prediction. It has to be remembered that in a Rapid Appraisal the data is not necessarily analysed for the production or testing of a theory, rather it serves a specific and limited purpose. For social scientists this limitation can be frustrating because rich sources of data are tapped, but not fully exploited. Yet, the data has to be surveyed thoroughly in order to arrive at valid definitions of areas of need, based on a clear understanding of the context within which these have arisen. Although the final product is not a scientific monograph, the analysis has to advance through certain stages in order to build up a systematic understanding of the data which forms the basis for drawing up the list of key concerns.

Triangulation

Before discussing the analysis of the three types of data, that is, secondary material, observational notations and interviews, we have to discuss the concept of triangulation. As outlined previously, Rapid Appraisal draws on a variety of research methods, resembling the design of multi-method research. According to Brewer and Hunter (1989) the particular attraction of this approach lies in the fact that a set of measures are employed whose indicators point to the same social phenomenon, but through the use of different data collection tools the risk of overlapping methodological biases is minimized. The deployment and comparison of the results of various measures in the same or nearly identical social situations is called triangulation. A further refinement is offered by Denzin (1978) who identifies the following types:

- data triangulation: the use of various data sources in one study;
- investigator triangulation: the use of different researchers within one study;
- theory triangulation: the use of multiple theoretical perspectives for the interpretation of one data set;
- methodological triangulation: the use of various methods to study one problem.

Janesick (1994) adds a further type, namely interdisciplinary triangulation which is defined as combining a range of disciplines within a single piece of research in order to broaden the understanding of both method and substance. Thus, Janesick proposes to go beyond traditional boundaries and includes art, dance, architecture alongside sociology, history or anthropology. The purpose of triangulation remains the same in all five types, that is to improve validity of the analysis.

In Rapid Appraisal three types of triangulation are used: first, data triangulation, whereby secondary data is compared with data drawn from places (geographical and social), individuals and groups. Second, investigator triangulation is applied, in particular, in the interviews where small sub-teams interview respondents. In the teams of two or three people, questioning and recording are rotated and thus each investigator has the opportunity to collect and analyse the data in various ways. Moreover, it could be argued that in certain cases interdisciplinary triangulation is exercised if investigators are drawn from different disciplinary backgrounds. For example, medical professionals collaborating with social work or psychology professionals. Third, methodological triangulation is used by drawing on both quantitative approaches, such as epidemiology and survey methods, and qualitative research, such as in-depth interviews. This can be schematically represented in Figure 6.1.

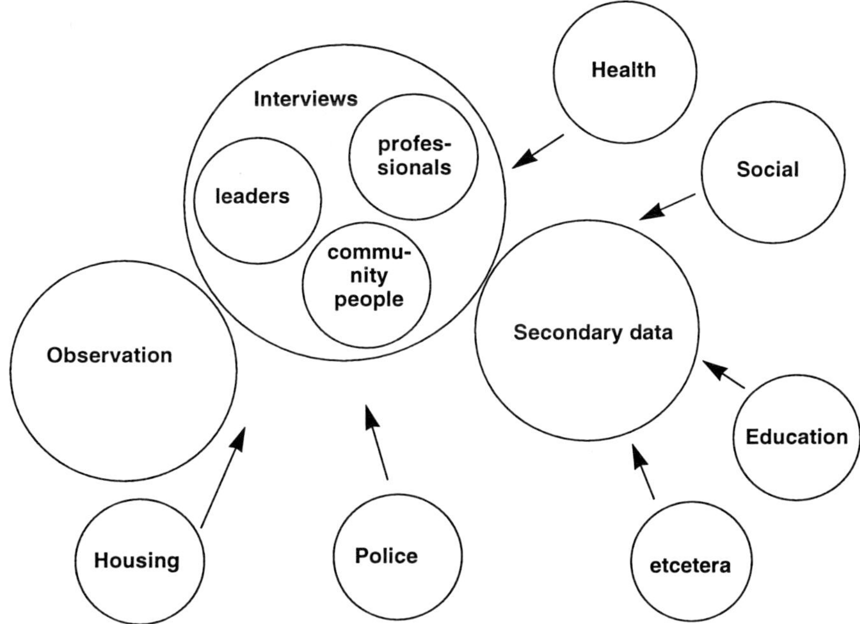

Figure 6.1 Triangulation.

Analysis of secondary data

The three main data sets collected in a Rapid Appraisal can be analysed separately before triangulation takes place. Secondary data has to be subjected to a common set of questions in order to establish its quality and whether it is 'fit for purpose'. This is particularly important in Rapid Appraisals as a diverse range of data is accessed, some designed according to scientific principles, other more in an *ad hoc* fashion. Dale and colleagues (1988) offer six key questions which assist in scrutinizing secondary data. While they focus on large data sets such as national surveys, their questions are relevant to the smaller scale set-up of a Rapid Appraisal:

- What was the purpose of the original study, for example, descriptive or explanatory, and does it, therefore, lend itself to re-analysis or not?
- What type of information has been collected, and does it cover the same topics necessary for the Rapid Appraisal?
- What kind of sampling frame is used? This will give some indication as to whether there is sufficient overlap with the Rapid Appraisal target population, and what the limitations are for use in the Rapid Appraisal.
- What are the credentials of the data which one wants to use? For example, if the data is collected by an established Census agency such as the British

Office of Population Censuses and Surveys, there is little doubt about the robustness of the material.

- Is the data representative for the population researched (this can apply to national data sets or locally collected information).
- When was the data collected and therefore, is it still relevant or should it be discarded?

The theoretical framework adopted in Rapid Appraisal is predominantly exploratory and secondary data will, as a result, be analysed to find patterns, regularities, deviant cases, and perhaps surprises. It serves a dual purpose of providing a general and descriptive background to the other data sets, and is used as a comparative touchstone in triangulation. The variety of the secondary material itself containing, for example, census data as well as narrative accounts, requires considerable discipline in testing quality and relevance. The above listed questions, combined with the design of an exploratory framework outlining the key parameters to be used, will strengthen this discipline.

A relatively straightforward method for ordering the secondary data analysis is described by Miles and Huberman (1994). They designed a document summary form which selects a finite range of points relevant to the analytical framework. Figure 6.2 illustrates their approach.

Miles and Huberman argue that the document summary helps to put the material within context, determines its significance and that it can be coded (much in the same way as the other material). The use of codes across all data sets facilitates the triangulation process and the formulation of community needs.

Analysis of observational data

Observation of people and social interactions figures largely in anthropology (mainly within naturalistic settings) and psychology (mainly in laboratory-type situations) where it is seen as a non-interventionist research strategy. As discussed previously, observation in Rapid Appraisal is less concerned with interactional patterns and social behaviour than with the environment within which individuals and communities live. In terms of analysis, a number of theoretical propositions have to be formulated which help to explore the relationship between humans and their environment. Within Rapid Appraisal, one of the key analytical concepts is equity, and this can be placed within broader conceptual frameworks which link health and environment. In the case of the urban milieu the WHO (1988b, 1989) has formulated a vision of the ecological city which encompasses four principles:

- minimum intrusion into the natural state: development and restructuring has to reflect the natural environment (climate, topography, vegetation, etc.);

Site: Rosehill.

Document number: 3.

Date received: June 25, 1995.

Name of document:
Annual report of the Beehive Club, 1994.

Event or contact with which document is associated (if appropriate):
Annual meeting, May 30, 1995.

Significance/importance of document:
Provides overview of activities of Beehive Club, operating in the Rosehill area.

Gives list of key people involved.

Brief summary of contents:
Number of children attending, age groups, addresses.

Number of children with special needs (and description of those needs).

Household composition (single/married parents, siblings, etc.)

Activities undertaken and level of participation.

Financial statement, including sources of funding.

Staffing (including volunteers), management structure.

Development plans (including business cases).

If this document is crucial to a particular contact attach it to write-up (e.g. interview) and file second copy in documents file.

Figure 6.2 Document summary form: annual report of playgroup. (After Miles and Huberman, 1994, p.55).

- maximum variety in the physical, social and economic structure of the city;
- closed system approach, optimizing the management of renewable resources;
- achieving an optimal balance between people and resources (physical, economic and cultural opportunities).

This framework can provide the anchor for the analysis of observational material through developing categories within the principles which order the observations. Miles and Huberman (1994) offer a rich variety of analytical tools, and for example, the conceptually ordered display could be employed here. For example, analysing equality of access to public transport resources could be displayed as shown in Table 6.5. This data display allows for salient features to be highlighted, which then lead to a summary of key issues to be checked against the other data sets in order to arrive at a list of needs, in this case concerning transport.

Table 6.5 Equality of access to public transport (the categories are illustrative only, and can be expanded or adapted

	Distance to home	Weekly costs in relation to income (%)	Fit with pattern of usage (time, flexibility)	Fit with need (access for disabled etc.)
Area 1 (high income)	Less than 1km	1.5%	Not accessible evenings	Little specific need, use own transport if necessary
Area 2 (middle income)	Between 0.5 and 1km from home	2%	Not sufficiently flexible for shift work	Difficult for elderly and disabled people
Area 3 (low income)	Between 0.5 and 1km from home	4% no concessions for unemployed people	Not sufficiently flexible, few day time buses for unemployed	Difficult for elderly and disabled people
Specific groups elderly people	Between 0.5–1 km from home. Still too far for disabled people	4–5% insufficient concessions for elderly and disabled people	Too few day time buses (high usage by elderly people)	Difficult, e.g. high steps, bus drivers do not always wait for people to sit down

Interesting methods have been reported from the developing world where different social or cultural groups have been asked to provide their own observations of the environment (Welbourn, 1991). For example, women and men draw maps of their neighbourhood emphasizing features that are important to their life experience, with women pinpointing access to water, shops, mills; while men locating meeting places and roads to the city. Parallels can be drawn to the developed world where parents of young children have different perceptions than elderly people about environmental hazards or places which are conducive to their social participation. Comparing the various perspectives within an observational analysis strengthens the understanding of the human–environment relationship and links it with social perceptions of the physical reality.

Analysis of interview data

The unstructured interviews that are carried out within the Rapid Appraisal for the first stage of generating issues pertaining to the list of community needs are a rich source of data. If a team of ethnographers were to analyse the data detailed accounts would ensue, based upon a sequence of coding, categorization, recognition of regularities and patterns (and deviant cases), the development of generalizations and concepts and finally theoretical statements. There is a large body of writing about the analysis of interview data, related to different theoretical positions. For example, the interpretivist approaches state that researchers are members of their own culture with its values and orientations, and this will be brought into the interview situation and its analysis. The distinction between the researcher and the researched is not neatly drawn, and has to be incorporated into the analysis. Another example originates in social anthropology where the main interest lies in uncovering and explaining the way in which people live their daily life (Van Maanen, 1979). The research process goes through a number of successive stages whereby material is constantly analysed before continuing to the next move in the field. A particular elaborated framework for analysis is the grounded theory approach by Glaser and Strauss (1967) where a constant dialectical movement between data and theory is sustained.

The purpose of Rapid Appraisal is less ambitious in that it seeks to formulate a number of key community concerns. However, it is possible to extrapolate from the social scientific models of analysis, and adopt the key stages in order to strengthen the validity of the analysis beyond anecdotal illustrations of people's perceptions of need. Miles and Huberman (1994) advocate three simple stages in the analytical process: namely data reduction, data display and conclusion drawing and verification. Data reduction is an integral part of the analysis where through the act of reduction researchers make analytical choices which are informed by both theory and the data. Data reduction can be achieved through coding, summarizing, organizing clusters, defining key themes and so on. Data display is a systematic attempt at ordering data so that conclusions can be drawn more easily from clearly assembled information. Miles and Huberman discuss a wide panoply of tools, including cognitive maps, matrices, charts, tables, networks and so on. Good displays allow the key features to 'jump off the page' (or the computer) and aid discovery of linkages, new insights and so on.

Drawing conclusions from the data emerges from noting regularities, patterns, explanations and propositions. Conclusions can be of different status, ranging from vague hunches, to theoretically grounded conclusions. In order to strengthen the conclusions verification plays an essential part. In Rapid Appraisal this takes two forms: within the interview material conclusions have to be checked against deviant cases so that the meaning is tested in terms of its plausibility and whether there is sufficient evidence to confirm it. Using several 'judges' to scan the same interview material further reinforces this process of verification. The second mode of verifying is through triangulation, as discussed previously. All data sets are compared with each other so that patterns, explanations and conclusions can be confirmed or refuted across the research material. Miles and Huberman define the triangulation activity very clearly: 'by seeing or hearing multiple *instances* of it from different *sources* by using different *methods* and by squaring the findings with others it needs to be squared with' (original emphasis) (1994, p.267).

Analysis of focus groups

Chapter 5 discussed methods of priority-setting using statistical or other techniques. Here we are going back one step, and look at the process predating the technical stage, namely, the dialogue about priorities through the use of focus groups. It has to be stated at the outset that focus groups are not the only method and, for example, the consensus conference (Stocking *et al.*, 1991) represents an alternative. The actual analysis of the data shows similarities with the analysis of the unstructured interview material, because focus group discussions provide similar in-depth material. At the same time, the structure of the material depends on the organization of the data collection, as focus groups generally adopt one of two strategies: a guided questioning route, with clear sequential markers for how an issue should be explored; or a more open-ended thematic route, where participants debate a particular issue in a relatively loose format. The first strategy facilitates analysis as an overall conceptual framework is already set up, and the priorities can be slotted into that framework. However, the discovery of alternative explanations is less likely, and verification is important in terms of testing the original design. The second strategy allows for new ideas to emanate from group discussions, but the analysis has to go through the more painstaking process of coding, patterning and concluding, described above.

Verification of the priority listing at the second stage is a crucially important stage in Rapid Appraisal. Validity has not only to be established in the methodological sense, but socially, that is with the community and organizational stakeholders. The key ethical issues centre around use of the results, benefits and costs, and ownership. Rapid Appraisal claims to involve communities in policy-making, and therefore, must take these ethical issues very seriously. The first step is to verify the results of the priority listing with the community in the widest possible sense, and we have earlier mentioned various ways of doing so, such as discussion groups, community surveys or public meetings. The degree of participation will provide insight into the degree of ownership felt by the community. This has to be matched by a similar feeling on the part of organizations and its decision-makers as they are key to implementation of the Rapid Appraisal findings. Lastly, openness must be established so that an honest assessment can be made about the benefits and costs of the Rapid Appraisal itself, and its possible consequences. This analysis forms a check on whether the aim of equity can be fulfilled, and whether the recommendations of the Rapid Appraisal are sustainable. The boundary between method and ethics in the analysis is consequently blurred, but it could be argued that they are intrinsically connected to the purpose of Rapid Appraisal.

CONCLUSION

In Rapid Appraisal a range of research methodologies are employed to collect a wide variety of material, and often the collection and analysis is carried out by a multi-disciplinary group of people. We have outlined the main methodological issues that have to be considered within Rapid Appraisal, and emphasized that, although the outcome of a Rapid Appraisal is primarily action-orientated rather than pure research, the conventions of good research can be observed. In a Rapid Appraisal the concept of triangulation is central in order to enhance the validity of the findings, and place the results of Rapid Appraisal against the quantitative material more commonly used in health policy and planning.

<table><tr><td>7</td><td># Change and continuity</td></tr></table>

The purpose of Rapid Appraisal is to influence health policy-making through the involvement of communities in setting priorities, which requires the commitment of resource holders to bring about change, reflecting community concerns. In the previous chapters the conceptual issues concerning the definition of communities, involvement and power sharing have been addressed, and methodological approaches relevant to Rapid Appraisal have been discussed. In this chapter the emphasis shifts to the strategic processes involved in changing health policy, and in particular the question of sustainability is a central feature. On the one hand, clarity is required as to the purpose and nature of change, appropriate targets, definition of roles and responsibilities and the commitment of resources; on the other hand, longer-term perspectives about empowerment at both grass roots and institutional levels have to be developed. These two issues will be discussed, and specific examples serve as an illustration of the solutions and dilemmas relating to the balance between change and continuity.

CHANGING POLICY AND STRATEGY

The origins of Rapid Appraisal can be traced back to the developing world where in the 1960s and 1970s academic theories and policy debates strongly emphasized underdevelopment and dependency themes. These theories influenced debates within health circles and centred around empowering the underprivileged, posing a challenge to established power structures. The theme of equity in health became dominant towards the end of the 1970s culminating in the Primary Health Care (PHC) approach initiated by the World Health Organization/UNICEF (1978). Many projects and grassroots initiatives had already embraced the thinking behind the PHC approach, building on community development and action research.

The work of Paulo Freire in Brazil has been one the most potent influences upon the re-orientation of health education in the developing world. Whilst his original research and practice centred around education, his philosophy extended to other spheres, because it questioned the fundamental institutions of society and the way in which they operated. Freire (1973) criticized the oppressive nature of education, and replaced it with a creative, questioning type of education which taught people a problem-seeking and problem-solving attitude to their environment. His empowerment philosophy involved people in identification of problems relevant to their own experience, to assess critically the social and historical basis of these problems and to develop strategies to overcome the obstacles in achieving the goals that they themselves have set in order to create a healthier society. Instead of individual-oriented education Freire advocated learning in groups in order to strengthen and support individual learning. The most important element in Freire's approach is to liberate people so that they can act as subjects (instead of being objects of oppression). The principles of Freire's participatory pedagogy fit well with the PHC approach, and have served to underpin both the strategies and practices of many projects over the last two decades.

The emphasis of much action-oriented work in health has been on change and the alleviation of inequities. As a corollary, change has been seen as going beyond the boundaries of health care and instead embracing a holistic concept of health, including change in the economic, social, cultural and psychological realm. Thus, the notion of multi-sectoral collaboration as the other plank of the PHC approach seems a logical extension of this thinking. Because of this wide focus it is understandable that the major preoccupation of people working in this field has been with effecting change, expressed in structural and power shifts. We have already discussed that power is not easily wrested from the hands of those who possess it (see Chapter 4). This does not mean that the theoretical point of equity and social justice is inaccurate, however, the reality of achieving these in practice should not be underestimated. The political and social actualities of the 1990s have forced both theoreticians and activists to revisit the strategies in pursuit of equity, and the agenda is being redefined.

Before embarking on that discussion, the foundation of Rapid Appraisal can be considered to lie within the tradition of community-based and participatory action. Kumar (1994) offers a bounded definition of Rapid Appraisal as applied research to 'facilitate a more rational decision-making process in real-life circumstances' (p.9), emphasizing that the success of the research depends on scientific criteria, but equally importantly on the relevance of the research to the problem. The definition of what constitutes a problem is firmly placed in the hands of those who are often ignored, and thus Rapid Appraisal takes a similar stance as Freire has done in his educational work. The bottom-up approach lies at the heart of Rapid Appraisal, but at the same time connects directly with the policy process. For this second aspect we have to turn to the contemporary development debates.

This discussion has to be preceded by drawing some parallels with the developed world. Hart and Bond (1995) provide a useful historical overview of action research in the UK and other Western countries. Rapid Appraisal is closely related to the thinking behind action research, and the points raised by Hart and Bond are relevant for contextualizing Rapid Appraisal. They situate the origins of action research in different traditions, including rational social management and Lewinian psychology, but the tradition most relevant to Rapid Appraisal is connected to the Community Development Projects (CDPs) of the late 1960s, which Hart and Bond argue are intimately bound up with the rediscovery of poverty. These projects were consistent with the bottom-up approach dominant in action research where communities, community workers and academic researchers jointly set the agenda and carried out the research. The fundamental shift in the definition of poverty paralleled the thinking discussed above in relation to Freire, namely that poverty was rooted in fundamental social and economic inequalities. Later on, action research was transposed to health education contexts with a similar emphasis on challenging power, in this case medical and bureaucratic power. As in the developing world, the focus was on change of structures of decision-making through empowerment of communities and disadvantaged groups. Hart and Bond pose the question in relation to the CDPs as 'to what extent it is possible through local initiatives to promote the kind of fundamental socio-economic change at national level that might be necessary to overcome such problems' (p.29). This question is very similar to the one posed in the paragraph above, namely the connection between change at local level and the policy process (either locally or nationally). It is this reality of not only broadening the scope of change, but also its sustainability that is exercising the mind of many people working in the areas of community involvement, development and institutional change.

SUSTAINABILITY

Kuhn (1970) has argued that scientific revolutions are often preceded by a sense of malfunctioning of an existing paradigm, which can lead to a crisis of that paradigm. In other words, once the explanatory power of a paradigm can be shown to be inadequate, and if the development is non-cumulative, there has to be revolutionary change in the sense that the old paradigm is to be wholly or partially replaced. This argument appears to hold true for the understanding of change, both in the developed and underdeveloped worlds of the 1990s. The momentous political and social changes resulting from the collapse of the old communist East bloc, the economic growth of repressive states such as South East Asian countries, the recession in the Western world and so on, have had a profound impact on theories of world order and the pursuit of equity. The relatively simple dichotomies used within development and dependency theories no longer appeared to square with the varied realities. The political strategies of fighting power from the outside (which lay at the heart of action research) did not deliver more than marginal changes, and thus never challenged established power structures or dominant thinking. For many people on the left whose allegiance continued to be with the underprivileged a Kuhnian paradigm crisis became inevitable in the 1990s.

Both in the developing and the developed world a new paradigm has emerged – representing for many a scientific revolution of sorts – which centres around a new consensus that the notion of sustainability holds the key. Sustainability is concerned with 'ensuring that people's basic needs are being met, that the resource base is conserved, that there is a sustainable population level, that environment and cross-sectoral concerns are integrated into decision-making processes and that communities are empowered' (World Commission on Environment and Development, 1987). Munslow and colleagues (1995) add that sustainable development is concerned with satisfying human needs and with improving the overall quality of life. The latter concept furthermore implies a longer time frame, in that not only the present quality of life, but that of future generations has to be safeguarded.

A number of issues, representing the paradigm shift can be highlighted: sustainability is concerned with trade-offs, rather than a wholesale taking over of power, and therefore has to negotiate the ways in which community concerns can be inserted within policy-making. As a result the purpose of bottom-up approaches not only to empower communities, but also to build their capacity to work with and within institutional frameworks. This has the danger of blunting the lay perspective, but on the other hand communities learn to recognize the political choices that must be made in a context of limited resources and competing demands. The ethics of decision-making can be enriched through the community perspective, and accountability becomes more real with communities positioned at the heart of the policy process. The concern with quality of life shifts the attention from inputs – equality of access – to resources, outputs and outcomes – the contribution that specific resource inputs actually make to the health and well-being of communities. Assessing those outcomes crucially depends on the judgement of communities and can no longer be the sole prerogative of experts.

Sustainability is no less complex as equity, and both the strategy and implementation of sustainable development require much thought and experimentation. Yet, it represents a fundamental change in thinking, calling into question the validity of the old dichotomies of capital and labour, centre and periphery, and moving towards more complex social divisions. Certainly, communities are not as easily defined (as we argued in Chapter 3) and the concept of networks which overlap and are dynamic (Crow and Allen, 1994) fits more easily with the notion of sustainability which is built around the diversity of communities and policy responses. One of the most difficult questions with regard to sustainability is the quality of institutional and community human resources. The premise that any change, and its continuation over time, depends on the human resource base underlies the concern with capacity building. This is a dual process in that institutions have to be able to manage major social transformations and require a range of skills to do so; communities have to understand the nature of transformation, their role within it and the way in which they can be involved in shaping policy. Only if both parties are confident about their own capacity, based upon information, training and knowledge of decision-making processes, can they be receptive to each other's perspectives. This requires, on the one hand, parallel processes of capacity building inside and outside institutions, but on the other hand establishing and maintaining dialogue and involvement of communities in decision-making. The alignment of these processes, and the related cultural changes required, are difficult and often generate resistance. The issue of control through shared ownership of the policy agenda is a particularly vexed one, and has been prominent in action research and similar participatory methods.

From a narrower vantage point and concerned with health care *per se*, Calnan (1995) has argued that there are good reasons to involve users and communities in decision-making. He argues that clinical effectiveness, efficiency and equity are important factors in determining the quality of health care, but that indicators of social acceptability of health care to citizens requires equal attention. The active contribution of individuals and social networks in the management of long-term medical and social care is important, as is their judgement on outcomes. Finally, ethical concerns mean that the users' perspective have to be taken into account. While some of Calnan's concerns operate at the individual rather than at the societal level, they underline the need to strengthen the knowledge and expertise of communities (and individuals within those) in order to be genuinely involved in decision-making processes, but also the need for decision-makers to know how to compare their perspectives with those of communities, and accord them equal value.

The emergence of this new, and more pragmatic agenda, means that action and participatory research methodologies have to be revisited. Community involvement in health policy continues to be an end in itself, yet, the strategic objectives have been reframed in terms of a continuing relationship with decision-makers rather than a short-term focus on change. It is the sustainability of these relationships, and the permanent input from below which help to make policies responsive and relevant. Saltman (1992) distinguishes between content and process democracy, with the former being a measure of formal political control over decisions in a particular subject area (through the medium of elections), while the latter means the direct participation of citizens in decision-making, both collectively and individually. Both concepts are important for the sustainability argument in that the structures for democratic participation have to be created, but at the same time mechanisms have to be present to give participation a voice through appropriate processes.

RAPID APPRAISAL AND SUSTAINABILITY

In order to achieve participation in the policy process, methodologies such as Rapid Appraisal have been in the ascendancy since the mid-1980s, because they emphasize the link between 'indigenous knowledge' (Kumar, 1994) and the making of policy. Furthermore, Rapid Appraisal engages in a process of negotiating an 'acceptable compromise' between various stakeholders (Marsden *et al.*, 1994), involving a range of moral and political agendas. Thus, Rapid Appraisal encompasses two main strands: first, it attempts to discover and describe social phenomena and processes, systematically explain their causes, and includes the interpretations of the various stakeholders; second, it also aims to describe the objective reality within which these processes occur. As a result, it must utilize a range of data sources which provide the information basis upon which the analysis of the perspectives of policy-makers and communities – especially including those groups whose views are generally overlooked – can be carried out. The collection of data, and the use of formal and informal, quantitative and qualitative methods, have already been discussed in Chapter 6. Here we focus on the inclusion of the relevant institutions, groups and individuals necessary for achieving the purpose of Rapid Appraisal, namely to instigate change, and secure its sustainability.

As argued previously, Rapid Appraisals start with the formation of a team drawn mainly from statutory organizations and from a variety of disciplines. The team must contain people who have control over resources, and people who can engage in longer term relationships with communities. The importance of the inclusion of resource holders is to ensure that the findings of a Rapid Appraisal can be implemented. More often than not resource holders are the people who can instigate policy changes, and commit the necessary resources to support change. Unless this is secured no fundamental or essential change can be achieved from a Rapid Appraisal, thus reducing it to a diagnostic exercise rather than realizing the goals of applying research for the benefit of communities. Equally important, however, is the question of continuity or, more accurately, sustainability. Many Rapid Appraisals managed to gain initial enthusiasm and momentum for change, considerably less were able to sustain this over time, and thus lost important credibility with local communities. Even more damaging is the communities' loss of faith in working with statutory organizations and institutions, thus precluding future collaborative ventures. It has been increasingly recognized that equal attention has to be paid to the issue of capacity building, both in institutions and within communities. In order to achieve this, Rapid Appraisals have begun to include more decision-makers who are willing to acknowledge the shortcomings in their own understanding, and the necessity to listen to communities' perspectives on priority needs. This can be considered as building capacity inside institutions as new skills of openness, accountability, valuing communities' experiential interpretations and so on have to be acquired. The institutional capacity to compare and contrast professional and managerial with lay knowledge can, as a result, enhance organizational effectiveness in responding to need.

Sustainability, however, does not tend to be guaranteed through the involvement of senior decision-makers. They are often people who are enthusiastic about the initiative, and see it as a platform from which they can communicate with communities and develop new policies. In reality, they have to cope with multiple demands, and cannot commit themselves to long-term relationships with one (or a few) communities as their remit tends to be wider. Thus, many Rapid Appraisals have incorporated middle and junior ranking people in organizations who have a more limited brief, which is often related to specific (geographically defined) communities. These are the professionals and managers who have more locally focused responsibilities and are more likely to display attitudes which are conducive to sustained dialogue with communities. The inclusion of this type of professional has proven to be crucially important for creating sustainable partnerships between institutions and communities.

The community is also a beneficiary of new knowledge through engagement in Rapid Appraisals. They will gain insight into institutional decision-making by being exposed to different logics, structures and political processes. It is important, if communities are to be equal and effective partners, that they understand the way in which policy is made, and the limitations placed upon decision-makers. They will see how the needs of their particular community have to be placed against the competing needs of other groups or communities, and must learn to make their case in a language that is acceptable within the policy context. A key problem in individuals learning to operate in these institutional frameworks is that they can become divorced from their communities if they are adopting the behaviours, language and power plays that are demanded within many institutional bureaucracies. The dilemma posed for many community 'activists' is that in order to be effective they have to play the right games, yet, not playing the same game is precisely the challenge that communities must pose to institutions. Gaining competence without sacrificing the purpose of community involvement is a difficult tightrope, and community solidarity is an important protection mechanism. The support that communities can give to people who are negotiating with institutions is crucially important, not only as a reference point, but also to widen the community's understanding of policy processes. Thus, capacity building operates both at the individual and the community-wide level, and requires robust community structures to exist.

The purpose of Rapid Appraisal and its specific use has to be clear from the outset if both change and continuity are to be on the agenda. Moreover, the scope of the Rapid Appraisal must be defined in order to set realistic boundaries on what the Rapid Appraisal can achieve. Both are important in determining the participants, thus paying due attention to the level of seniority, the range of skills, and the extent of the responsibilities of institutional team members. The range of people to be interviewed from the community, and the people to be involved in a programme of change requires equally careful consideration in terms of their scope of knowledge and influence, their credibility and representativeness, their ability and willingness to engage in a dialogue with policy-makers. In order to secure the commitment from both sides, one has to return to the foundations of Rapid Appraisal:

- it has to be rapid, ensuring that findings and recommendations are timely and quickly available to decision-makers. This is particularly important in relation to the rapport and credibility that can be built up between institutions and communities through quick action;
- it has to be an appraisal which reflects the concerns of communities and the diversity within those communities;
- it has to be flexible allowing the exploration of new ideas and options, tapping the creativity of all stakeholders, and creating long-term and sustainable relationships which facilitate the exploitation of this creativity;
- Kumar (1994) adds a fourth dimension, namely low costs. It can be argued that Rapid Appraisals are cheap in comparison to sample surveys, and in terms of actual money being paid. As we have argued previously, Rapid Appraisals are not cheap when opportunity costs are calculated, that is, managerial and community time during and following Rapid Appraisals. However, without proper cost-effectiveness analysis the true costs and benefits of Rapid Appraisals cannot be established with certainty, but appear to be good value for money in instituting rapid change, and building capacity.

Example of change

The Rapid Appraisal exercise carried out in Highfields in 1989 pointed out that the consequences of poverty were high on the priority listing. While poverty itself was difficult to address directly as it was closely bound up with high regional levels of unemployment, and a dearth of new opportunities, the community felt that alleviating poverty remained high on their agenda. One of the key issues was poor nutritional intake, in particular among young children. There were few shops in the area that sold cheap, fresh food and the large supermarkets were situated in the city centre, a bus ride away. The choices for young parents were limited: either they bought inferior quality food locally, and at higher expense, or they bought better and cheaper food at the supermarkets, but had to travel on public transport. Because of their limited budgets they could often not take advantage of bulk purchase offers, nor could they physically carry large amounts of shopping on the bus.

With the support from the Local Authority a development worker was assigned to help the community to establish a food co-operative. The project was started with one of the mother and toddler groups who had voiced the original problem very clearly. The worker trained the group in organizational skills, fund-raising, budgeting and accounting. A rota was set up for groups of three women to buy or order the food (while their children were looked after by the rest of the group). The Health Authority freed up one of the dieticians to advise the group on buying nutritious and economic foodstuffs, and to demonstrate creative ways in which to prepare meals for families. Space was found in the community centre to store supplies and the kitchen was utilized for the sessions with the dietician. After six months the group was self-sufficient, and began to plan setting up a credit union for buying household appliances. The input of the two professionals was reduced from 20% of their time to an occasional visit, and being on hand for advice.

In this example the target for change was clearly delineated and a time frame was agreed. The roles and responsibilities of community people and professionals respectively were defined, and senior managers committed the resources for the development worker and the dietician to work on a sessional basis on the project. A transfer of skills such as running a co-operative was an important objective, and could be considered to be successful when the group themselves started to plan for the credit union.

Example of sustainable development

The Bridgemere Rapid Appraisal which took place in 1993 emphasized the problems of urban deprivation, placing the problems associated with unemployment as high priorities. It also focused on the needs of elderly people, single parent families and the young (particularly teenagers) and specific issues such as homelessness and unsafe environments. A Health Forum was established following a high profile presentation of the Rapid Appraisal findings, including most statutory agencies (and people from the original Rapid Appraisal team), local councillors and community representatives. The Health Forum operates as a body where a permanent dialogue between the community and institutions can take place, and where action plans are instigated and evaluated.

One of the important initiatives coming from the Health Forum focuses on capacity building in the community. The issues which required sustained action were numerous, and could not be addressed by using professional inputs alone. The idea of developing the 'lay health worker' concept, drawing on understanding health in its widest meaning, originated from the community itself. Other examples from the UK and abroad were used to develop the local idea of recruiting local people and training them to work in a number of areas such as the establishment of support groups for frail elderly people, for people who suffer from depression and for unemployed individuals. Local workers could also operate in health promotion activities such as smoking cessation and controlling alcohol intake. A further idea was to use local people to strengthen professional activity in the areas of leisure activity development, safety schemes and postnatal support. The establishment of such a wide range of initiatives helped the local community to acquire or strengthen internal skills, and at the same time to work with institutions and professionals to set locally appropriate agendas and standards.

Unlike in the first example, the Rapid Appraisal did not emphasize immediate change, rather to build up structures which made a continuing dialogue possible between the community and statutory organizations around policy and planning. From that platform a range of projects have been formulated which are intended to have a longer-term time frame and focus on the capacity building within the community. The time element, however, had to be carefully managed as too long a gap (more than six months on average) would have meant losing the momentum gathered through the Rapid Appraisal exercise.

The purpose of change in this Rapid Appraisal focused on institutional development through setting up the Health Forum, and the roles and responsibilities for community members and statutory organizations were defined within that framework. From that basis, capacity building within the community became a key objective, which required input from professionals in terms of skills training. Outside funding had also to be sought for creating a physical basis for the lay health workers and their operational costs. The community was centrally involved with writing bids, thus building up their knowledge of project proposals and negotiating with funding bodies. While the emphasis was on the long-term development of community capacity, a balance had to be found with quick delivery, and the Health Forum remained an important vehicle for implementing change which needed statutory support.

8 | **Evaluating Rapid Appraisal**

Rapid Appraisals have been carried out over the last decade in many different contexts, with many different groups of people and with a diverse set of objectives. To date, there has been no systematic evaluation of their effectiveness, and only anecdotal evidence exists about the success of specific programmes. This lacuna is not necessarily the result of a lack of interest in or an unwillingness to engage in evaluation. More often than not evaluations are not systematically planned to be included at the start of a Rapid Appraisal, and because of its action orientation and short time frames, evaluation does not sit comfortably within a Rapid Appraisal project. Judging the outcome of a Rapid Appraisal requires one to look at the effects over time, rather than just focusing on the immediate impact of change. Yet, if Rapid Appraisal is to prove that it can deliver both change and sustainability, a more systematic approach to evaluation has to be instigated.

In this chapter we will discuss the principles of evaluation as applied to health programmes such as Rapid Appraisal. From the available evidence we will then outline some of the gains and limitations of Rapid Appraisal and discuss where evidence has to be strengthened in order to support its claims. Finally, it is important to address the future of Rapid Appraisal, and in particular, how it connects with some of the research and development activity in the field of visioning for health. The research on alternative futures has become increasingly important as a policy development tool, and as a way of creating alternative ways of involving communities. Rapid Appraisal can connect with this expanding field of inquiry, and we will explore some tentative ideas.

EVALUATING HEALTH PROGRAMMES

Like many other terms, evaluation has multiple interpretations depending on the theoretical perspective of the researcher. Within health there are two strong influences on the way evaluation is defined. The first one is derived from the medical model and states that evaluation is 'the critical assessment, on as objective basis as possible, of the degree to which entire services or their component parts fulfil stated goals' (St. Leger *et al.*, 1992, p.1). The authors emphasize first, the centrality of the notion that evaluation requires comparison with a standard, which may be absolute or comparative, and second, the need for objectivity of findings, that is, to be independent of the judgements and prejudices of the evaluators and/or those who commissioned the evaluation. This approach to evaluation may be appropriate to clinical settings, but certainly would not be adequate in the case of programmes such as Rapid Appraisal, because no standard of health and inequality can be defined in absolute terms. The notion of objectivity is generally subordinate in Rapid Appraisal where instead reliance is placed upon intersubjectivity and the social construction of ideas and values.

The second influence on evaluation research comes from the social sciences. In relation to health, Fink (1993) defines evaluation as follows: 'Programme evaluation is a diligent investigation of a programme's characteristics and merits. Its purpose is to provide information on the effectiveness of projects so as to optimize the outcomes, efficiency and quality of health care. Evaluations can analyse a programme's structure, activities, and organization and examine its political and social environment. They can also appraise the achievement of a project's goals and objectives and the extent of its impact and costs' (p.2). This definition is consistent with many others emanating from social science-based evaluations, and in particular from those relating to participatory projects (Marsden and Oakley, 1991) which emphasize the need to include accountability upwards (to institutions and resource holders) and downwards (to communities). A detailed discussion of the evaluation approaches found in health services research is presented elsewhere (Ong, 1993). For the purpose of this chapter we will focus more narrowly on the concept that evaluation in Rapid Appraisal has to take account of the diverse perspectives on the aims and objectives of Rapid Appraisal, and the various social constructions of outcomes. The evaluation of Rapid Appraisal could be incremental, namely that accumulated evidence from different Rapid Appraisal exercises provides evidence for both the effectiveness of individual projects, and the method generally.

Commonly, evaluations address the issues of structure, process, outcome and impact. The distinction between the latter two is in terms of time scale and scope: outcome relates to the achievement of immediate objectives, while impact relates to the broader and longer-term effects of achieving those specific objectives. When evaluating Rapid Appraisals the issue of structure can be addressed through examination of its purpose, whether it primarily serves as a diagnostic tool, or whether it focuses on formulating actions. Furthermore, the scope of the Rapid Appraisal is important, because too often this is defined too narrowly. For example, by just focusing on health or medical services, or on specific client groups. Rapid Appraisal is intended to be holistic, and this determines the structure through the incorporation of a wide spectrum of stake-holders from the formal and informal sectors.

The other issue in relation to structure is the context within which Rapid Appraisal is taking place. With its focus on community perspectives, comparative material from other communities, national, regional and local strategies, specific policies for achievement of targets and so on have to be taken into account as they partially determine the boundaries to a Rapid Appraisal. A full appreciation of the structural context, and the external forces which shape a Rapid Appraisal is necessary in order to evaluate its outcome.

Following from the above, the structure is also determined by the involvement of particular institutions and individuals. The breadth of organizational input, the level of seniority of resource holders, the range of people who can provide continuity, are some of the key factors which structure a Rapid Appraisal. This team of people will also define the parameters for the Rapid Appraisal and its general purpose. The structure of the team influences the access to the community, the way in which a dialogue can be framed and how a Rapid Appraisal can be actioned. All of these issues have to be addressed in the evaluation of each Rapid Appraisal.

The process has to be documented in detail in order to provide evidence of the methods used to access the community and to elicit their views. Representativeness of the sample and the quality of the interviews (for example, consistency, depth and comprehensiveness) are key issues. The quality of the secondary data and observational material has equally to be evaluated against explicit criteria, because taken together all this material forms a baseline against which future action plans can be assessed in terms of health improvement. Triangulation will be a major tool, but transparency of documentation remains essential so that the data can be scrutinized by independent outsiders.

A further check on the process is to investigate whether the respondents, and especially those from the community, feel that their views are adequately reflected (not synonymous with being acted upon). This can be done through independent review or built into the research process by providing the respondents with drafts of the needs listing, to validate the priority listing through cross-checking and to provide respondents with drafts of the recommendations. The additional advantage is to give the community more control over the Rapid Appraisal process through allowing feedback at all relevant stages.

The measurement of outcomes in clinical research has been an area of debate and has received much attention in current health discussions as it relates to effectiveness and cost-effectiveness. In Rapid Appraisal we are not searching for similar formal measurements, rather we are looking for descriptive indicators as to whether the objectives of the Rapid Appraisal have been met. This does not necessarily exclude quantifiable data, and for example morbidity or service usage data can provide evidence of the effectiveness of Rapid Appraisal.

However, in general, evaluation of Rapid Appraisal will rely on varied data sources and can be likened to Fazey's (1987) model which targets different levels: individual; the programme itself; the service system(s) of which the programme is part; and society as a whole. This is consistent with the purpose of Rapid Appraisal in that it is holistic, and focuses on individuals and groups within society and the way in which service systems can take a part in improving their well-being.

Concretely, the type of questions to be asked are whether the objectives of a Rapid Appraisal have benefited individuals and groups, and how? This will have to be investigated through both formal data sources, and comparing them against a baseline, and through the perspectives of the stakeholders. The question of how service systems, that is, participating institutions have responded – by contributing or not to action plans – will be next on the agenda, and possibly wider effects can be detected (even though it is unlikely to be at the level of society as a whole). One of the key points to include is that outcomes are defined differently by different stakeholders, precisely because they are contextualized by their belief systems and expectations. Thus, the so-called objective view of benefit cannot be achieved, not in the least because Rapid Appraisal emphasizes people's subjectivity. Many social scientists argue that this ethnographic approach strengthens the evaluation and allows for communities to participate in the assessment. Marsden and colleagues (1994) argue that solutions should be context-specific and focus on the development of community capacity to utilize and absorb external resources. Therefore, evaluation cannot be a top-down, formal scientific approach, but has to be consistent with the philosophy of Rapid Appraisal, and include the diverse realities of both recipients (i.e. communities and individuals) of resource inputs and institutions.

Measuring impact requires a long time horizon which appears to contradict the rapidity of Rapid Appraisal. However, if sustainability is to be an objective, than this has to be evaluated in a systematic manner. The baseline measures of relative deprivation, morbidity and mortality provide the background to this longitudinal perspective. The collection of qualitative data within the community needs to be repeated after an agreed interval, for example, when a specific action plan has been implemented, delivered its intended outcomes and has become embedded in the community. Key stakeholders in the community and various institutions have to be included in an impact analysis in order to arrive at a multi-faceted evaluation.

Example

The Highfields food co-operative discussed in Chapter 7 could be examined again after two years to elicit the community's and professionals' views on its continuing influence on nutrition, and whether it has effected further initiatives to improve the well-being of children and families. Parents (and children) need to be interviewed, alongside GPs, health visitors, school nurses, dieticians, community workers and other relevant professionals. The quantitative data on children's growth and development could be assessed by local health workers and compared with the original baseline data. Issues such as dental decay and school performance could be included in order to provide a wider context to the evaluation.

STRENGTHS AND LIMITATIONS OF RAPID APPRAISAL

Throughout the previous chapters many of the strengths and limitations of Rapid Appraisal have been addressed implicitly. It is important at this point to summarize those, so that an indication can be given as to the direction in which Rapid Appraisal can be developed, and how it connects with the ideas about futures and leadership within communities and institutions.

Summary analyses of the contribution of Rapid Appraisal have been carried out on applications in varied settings and fields of inquiry (Kumar, 1994) and in the health arena (Rifkin, 1992). Both evaluations focus on the method itself and emphasize its value as a quick approach to information collection by professionals, through the involvement of communities in the process. As Rapid Appraisal uses a specific set of activities, namely the collection of quantitative and qualitative data, within a limited time frame, the process is not only quick, but also relatively low cost, and is particularly useful for planning at local levels. By working closely with communities, the type of information normally ignored in planning – namely an in-depth understanding of a community's beliefs and value systems – can be accessed and integrated into the decision-making process. The direct dialogue between communities and resource holders allows the accountability of decision-makers to be more transparent, and stimulates the implementation of findings. Finally, Rapid Appraisal offers a flexible approach which can be adapted to local circumstances, and which can accommodate a wide range of methodologies. Chambers (1992) provides a comprehensive list of methods, their appropriateness for specific problems or questions, and their particular strengths. For example, participatory mapping and modelling can focus on people (demography), social structures, community facilities, local hazards and service utilization. These methods are useful for establishing rapport with a community, provide insight into the demographic structure and vulnerable groups within the community, can identify risk factors and so on.

While many of the strengths have been illustrated in this book, it is important to be aware of the limitations of Rapid Appraisal as this helps to prevent it being used for the wrong reasons, with ill-formed objectives or within a context which is not conducive to its success. Rapid Appraisal is a holistic method and does not lend itself easily to examining narrowly defined health services issues. For example, to look at children's dental health services requires a different method than Rapid Appraisal, probably combining clinical research with in-depth qualitative interviews with a sample of parents and children.

The multi-agency, multi-disciplinary approach is fundamental to Rapid Appraisal and cannot be compromised, and while this is one of its main strengths, it is also a potential weakness. First, it will be difficult to secure the involvement of a wide range of institutions and individuals, but most importantly, considerable persuasion is required to gain commitment of resources and collaboration over an extended period of time. It is essential, however, that this level of commitment is clarified from the start, otherwise the intended actions and change cannot be delivered. The detrimental effects on community participation in policy formulation immediately and in the long term should not be underestimated.

The use of qualitative methods and data collection in policy and planning is still far from widely accepted, and in the health field, constant comparison is made with natural science methods. Although this is slowly changing, and awareness of the particular contribution of qualitative research is becoming recognized (Pope and Mays, 1995), approaches such as Rapid Appraisal have to be vigilant about a range of methodological issues. The most important ones are reliability and validity, and in Chapter 6 we have outlined the significance of careful sampling, triangulation and reducing bias in analysis. The findings must be scientifically robust and transparent, whilst simultaneously emphasizing the particular nature and strength of ethnographic material. The complementarity of methods used in Rapid Appraisal constitutes its particular attraction and thus the potential 'liability' of qualitative material can be turned into a strength when it demonstrates how it elucidates and enriches the quantitative data.

The level of generalization possible from a Rapid Appraisal is limited, and it is important to recognize that the focus of Rapid Appraisal is on relatively small communities, and provides a snapshot in time. The time element can be extended by developing a longitudinal research design. The representativeness of a community can be extended through detailed comparison with similar communities, but this cannot be taken as far as with quantitative methods. While the credibility of Rapid Appraisal findings are not primarily based upon statistical evidence, its credence in terms of experiential accounts is not in doubt. The balance between the two sets of evidence has to be carefully managed in order to convince decision-makers.

No research approach is perfect. Rapid Appraisal must be used within the appropriate context, and for the right purpose, in order to optimize its strengths and limit its weaknesses. Because of its flexibility, Rapid Appraisal has the advantage that methodological innovations and improvements can be made continuously and the examples from this book and elsewhere (Kumar, 1993; the publication of the Notes on Participatory Learning and Action – formerly RRA Notes) are testimony to the creativity of communities and research teams.

RAPID APPRAISAL AND FUTURES RESEARCH

The World Health Organization has continually evaluated the progress of its Health for All by the Year 2000 strategy (WHO, 1993) and in particular the advances in Primary Health Care. Progress has been uneven, although commitment to the principles is strong world-wide. The economic disparities between and within countries are widening, thus endangering the health and well-being of populations. This global situation has led the WHO (1992) to revisit its fundamental approaches, and in particular public health action. A key stimulus for new thinking is the field of futures research, and the manner in which it connects with the HFA 2000 philosophy: 'Our vision for health for all captures fundamental concerns for building lasting peace through social development. The principles of health for all express our yearning for a world where all peoples and individuals have access to effective and affordable health care. It is an aspiration for equity in health opportunities; its represents a quest for social justice' (Nakajima, in Taket, 1993, p.v).

Health futures research is a relatively new field, and is concerned with providing 'a set of tools that allow more effective exploration of *what might happen* and they help us clarify *what we want to happen*, what we want to create' (authors' emphasis) (Bezold and Hancock, 1993). Bezold and Hancock make a distinction between different types of futures:

- Possible futures: all things that may possibly happen, however unlikely. For example, science fiction or everyone staying young forever through medical interventions.
- Plausible futures: what could happen, given our present understanding. This can include discrete forecasts or a set of scenarios (see below). For example, the shift of all but emergency and high-cost health care to the community.
- Probable futures: what is most likely to happen, based upon an interpretation of the present and an appraisal of likely trends and developments. For example, the growth of the elderly population and the increase of the dependency ratio.
- Preferable future: the one future we would like to have happen, which involves a vision of a future we want to create. For example, the elimination of inequalities in health.

In order to think creatively about the future, all the above four types have to be taken into account, but Bezold and Hancock argue that it is particularly fruitful to compare probable and preferable futures. The parallel can be drawn between comparing planning with strategy, in that the former tries to build incrementally on the present, and make it predictable; while the latter encourages formulation of a vision of a desirable future, and taking control over how the present can help to create that future. For a future to be 'normative', that is to set values about social life, the involvement of broad sections of the population is required so that a social consensus can be reached about both the direction of, and commitment to, that vision of the future. This is an important connection with Rapid Appraisal which is predicated upon the empowerment of people and communities in realizing change. Defining preferable futures is an extension of Rapid Appraisal in that it can secure its sustainability and stimulate development into a coherent strategy. The second connection between health futures and Rapid Appraisal is that both define health in its widest sense, and consider health care as but one part of the improvement in health. As such they are part of the same continuum of working towards HFA 2000, and have mutually reinforcing approaches.

The methods used in futures work are both quantitative and qualitative, and we will outline the most commonly used approaches. The first is represented by trends, which are defined as patterns of change over time, have predictive value because they can show developments from the past to the future. Formulating trends can be based upon quantitative material, such as demographic data or clinical research data (with or without computer modelling) combined with qualitative assessment of that data through techniques such as Delphi. For example, the Welsh Health Planning Forum carried out an analysis of the future relationship between hospital and primary care using predictions of demographic change to the year 2002, predicted numbers of people with specific diagnoses, an assessment of the development of medical technology and expert judgements about effectiveness and future developments in medical interventions (using the Delphi approach), in order to model the balance of services for the future (Warner *et al.*, 1993).

The above exercise also used a scenario approach, which is a second key tool for health futures. Scenarios were developed by Shell as a device to focus strategy and concrete decision-making (Boezeman, 1986). Scenarios are descriptions of a possible future, and provide an internally consistent picture of that future. They also take a broad perspective, encompassing economic, social, cultural and technical development. Most importantly, alternative scenarios (usually best and worst cases) have to be developed to stimulate creative thinking about concrete decisions. Scenario development for health has received government support in the Netherlands and from the mid-1980s it played a central role in health strategy formulation through the work of the Steering Committee on Future Health Scenarios, resulting in publications on a wide range of diseases, technologies and public health issues. For example, the report on chronic diseases (STG, 1992) generated four scenarios, each describing how the numbers of patients, the prevalence and level of disease and complications, the quality of life and service usage differed under the four different scenarios. This comparison then clarified the choices available for present and future policy.

Another example of the application of scenarios at a national level is the Crossroads report from Sweden (Federation of Swedish County Councils, 1992). The point of departure for this exercise was the perspective of the citizen, namely the public's assessment of health care delivery, and the perceptions of care givers (both formal and informal) of the structural features which limited or prevented the fulfilment of the demands and expectations of citizens. The scenarios were used as conceptual models which assisted the description of changes that needed to be made to health care delivery, and the political processes which would facilitate this change. The Crossroads project developed three scenarios: first, a national model with wide freedom of choice and a developed social market; second, a co-ordinated model where care delivery and health insurance of working people were co-ordinated, and where health care and social services were co-ordinated for young people and pensioners; third, a population-based model which was highly structured and operated at a regional co-ordination level. Again, as in the Dutch case, the three scenarios generated a range of policy options which were brought together into a more coherent health strategy.

The third key tool in health futures is visioning. McNerney (1992) defines a vision as a description of a future we want to create (that is, a preferable future), so that we have to rethink and redesign existing models, procedures and systems. In this way it represents a radical and creative model for strategic planning. An example of an ambitious and global visioning exercise is Celebration Health (Bezold *et al.*, 1993). The town of Celebration in Florida served as a prototype for formulating a vision of health and health care in the 21st century. An international group of 'futurists' came together in a three-day symposium and formulated the design principles for 21st century health systems. Its key objectives to generate health were to reduce preventable disease and lower the costs of health care by two-thirds; to establish clear links to community needs; and to promote healthy companies (workplaces). The resulting framework for health care delivery emphasized equity (accessibility and availability), integration and collaboration; holism (mental and physical well-being); innovation; adaptability and flexibility (local responsiveness); cost-effectiveness.

Similar, more focused exercises have been carried out in Wales with the publication of the Pathfinder documents which offer a ten year vision of health and health care, based upon an integrated strategy (Welsh Office, 1992); and in England, where a vision of integrated health and social care was presented in a discussion paper called 'Caring for the community in the 21st century' (GCL and HSMU, 1992). All these visioning projects have taken a number of value statements as the basis for their preferred future, and then built up a logical and internally consistent model of health and delivery of care. The methods used for these large- and medium-scale exercises can be adapted for local use.

The key elements in futures research pertinent to Rapid Appraisal are the new participative avenues and partnerships between policy-makers and communities. For visions to be capable of guiding strategy they have to be owned by policy-makers, but also by the public. In order to achieve this wide ownership visions have to be generated by and shared between institutions and communities. An important ingredient in managing the tension between a vision, which can be perceived as lofty or removed from current reality, is the role of leaders. These are leaders in organizations as well as in the community, who have to stimulate visions, possess charisma and can mobilize people. In Rapid Appraisal both sets of leaders are identified, and have been tied into the process from the beginning, that is, making a diagnosis of the community, through to the process of implementing change. Visioning appears to be a logical extension of this trajectory by building on change and transforming this into a coherent and incremental approach towards a desired future. The dialogue initiated in the earlier phases of the Rapid Appraisal can be extended to engage into consensus building about a vision for the community, and determining the contribution of organizations to turn that future into reality. Again, likewise as in implementing the findings of the Rapid Appraisal, joint responsibilities for actioning specific steps in the strategy can be allocated so that the collaborative structures between institutions and communities continue to be exploited and enhanced.

The WHO document (1993) contends that health futures studies play a continuing and important role in achieving the HFA 2000 objectives. These type of studies have to be capable of envisioning health for different cultures, communities and subgroups and therefore, must be public and participative. While futures research reveals people's dreams and aspirations, it simultaneously uncovers vested interests which can halt the achievement of, for example, equity or community participation. The challenge is to mobilize all stakeholders to subscribe to the same agenda from which each can benefit. This means that the ethical content (i.e. the values underlying the vision) has to be explicit and negotiated on. Rapid Appraisal has started this process by making choices, setting priorities and debating the value basis of these choices. The development of a long-term vision takes this journey into the ethics of decision-making one step further, and should bring communities closer to achieving health and health gain in an equitable manner.

Planning a vision exercise

The Health Forum in Bridgemere has decided on visioning as the next logical step from their Rapid Appraisal two years ago. The Rapid Appraisal recommendations, and the evaluation of the action plans implemented thus far are taken as point of departure for a visioning workshop so that a baseline of current health and well-being can be set. The Health Forum, strengthened by further community participants, is planning a day in which they will put together their individual dreams into one vision for Bridgemere to the year 2005. This vision will then be distributed to the community through existing groups and informal meetings to be debated and refined.

Once the health vision has gained wide support a small working party with membership of the community and resource holders (which could overlap with the Health Forum, or be a reconstituted Forum) will then be charged with deconstructing the vision into a series of linked objectives and targets, which in turn have to be broken down into chronological actions, and defined roles and responsibilities. The actions have to be evaluated against the overall strategic framework, and their contribution to the overall vision has to be regularly assessed. The full range of quantitative and qualitative methodologies for estimating progress has to be deployed, and community participation in both the implementation and continuous assessment must be secured, for example, through regular workshop sessions with community leaders, interest groups and so on. These meetings are intended to ascertain whether the community continues to support the direction of the vision and the related actions so that the vision can actually be achieved.

Doing a Rapid Appraisal – the practical issues   9

This chapter offers a do-it-yourself overview of the various steps in a Rapid Appraisal, and summarizes the discussion from the previous chapters. It will not go into detail into any of the theoretical issues, but only refer to them as and when necessary, and instead focus on the operational issues involved in every stage of a Rapid Appraisal. As argued previously, the Rapid Appraisal method is not written in tablets of stone, but is an evolving methodology. It can be changed according to local circumstances such as the availability of people, skills and resources. Yet, there are a number of principles which set it apart from other community-based methodologies, and it is recommended to follow those principles as closely as possible.

It has to be remembered that a Rapid Appraisal cannot be carried out in a vacuum, and needs to be complemented by other methodologies which provide a broader and comparative perspective, often based upon larger samples and quantitative data. Most importantly, a Rapid Appraisal can only be successfully applied if the policy context is conducive, that is, when there is commitment from resource holders to actually implement some of the findings of the Rapid Appraisal. This logically leads us to discussing the first step.

STEP 1. DEFINING PURPOSE, TARGET COMMUNITY AND AGENCIES INVOLVED

It is crucial to be clear about the purpose of a Rapid Appraisal, and situate it within the local context. Thus, if the Rapid Appraisal is predominantly seen as a diagnostic tool this has to be made clear to all participants, and in particular to the local community, because the implementation phase is, of necessity, not directly related to the results of the Rapid Appraisal. If the Rapid Appraisal is viewed as a tool to understand priority needs and to inform policy, a clear commitment to implementation has to be secured from key stakeholders, both from resource holders in statutory and voluntary organizations, and from the community itself. If the Rapid Appraisal is considered as a tool to secure long-term collaboration with the community due consideration has to be given to the stability of key personnel deployed from organizations in order to sustain relationships between resource holders and communities. Of course, the three purposes can co-exist together, and a balance has to be found between the three objectives.

Often the selection of the target community is done top-down. However, there have been occasions where a local community, or people working within a community, requested a Rapid Appraisal to be carried out. One of the key considerations in deciding upon a Rapid Appraisal is to afford a voice for communities which have traditionally not been able to access decision-making processes. Thus, most commonly, relatively deprived communities have been involved in Rapid Appraisals. In order to select communities, a preliminary analysis of available data is carried out, establishing relative disadvantage on the basis of, for example, census statistics, service usage, minority groupings or specific knowledge about health and social problems. A subjective analysis can be carried out asking community people themselves whether they feel a Rapid Appraisal exercise would be helpful to improving the quality of life for the community. Most importantly, the parameters of the community have to be defined, whether these are geographic, cultural or otherwise. Testing these parameters out locally is an important element in the Rapid Appraisal.

The involvement of agencies in the Rapid Appraisal team depends on local circumstances, and a choice has to emerge from the preliminary analysis of available data. Depending on the issues which can be tentatively described from this analysis, the range of agencies can be defined, and there are no set rules as to who can or cannot be involved. Thus, participation can range from health and social services, to probation, police, specific voluntary agencies and so on. The final phase of implementation and sustainability has, of course, to be kept in mind and the organizations have to be assessed in terms of their ability and commitment to deliver in the short and long term.

STEP 2. THE PREPARATION OF THE RAPID APPRAISAL

In most cases the Rapid Appraisal is instigated by one person or a small team, who act as 'dynamizers' for the whole process. The preparation of the Rapid Appraisal consists of gathering together team members. This is often difficult because the team members have to be people who are resource holders and these individuals often are senior managers or professionals who are extremely busy. They have to be convinced of the appropriateness and usefulness of the

Rapid Appraisal in terms of delivering short-term goals, and as a long-term investment in a community. The time commitment required of these people tends to be interpreted as a large opportunity cost (that is, an average of ten working days) but this has to be considered against the possibility of both direct project gains (the explicit goals of a Rapid Appraisal) and indirect gains in the form of collaborative working across agencies and different professional disciplines. The dynamizers are charged with 'selling' the project to the different organizations and individuals within them.

A typical Rapid Appraisal team consists of 10–12 people from different organizations and disciplinary backgrounds. The objective of achieving change can be met if the team contains a number of senior people who have control over key budgets. The objective of sustaining collaborative relationships with communities is possibly best met by including team members who by virtue of their professional role can remain in regular contact with communities.

STEP 3. THE WORKSHOP

The purpose of the workshop is to bring together the various team members in order to agree the main objectives of the Rapid Appraisal exercise, the method of work and to create a team. An example of a workshop programme is given in Fig. 9.1.

Setting the objectives of a Rapid Appraisal has to be done against the background of other work on needs assessment and community involvement, and the various organizational strategies and policies. Thus, it is important to arrive at an agreed understanding of the context and limitations of the Rapid Appraisal.

The discussion about the target area or community requires sufficient time, because again, agreement has to be reached as to what criteria are used for deciding upon a particular community, and whether this delineation can be underpinned with evidence. The evidence can be quantitative, based on the specific problems which are documented, or can be qualitative, based on accounts of the community itself as to how they define their identity. Determining the exact boundaries for the target community is best done with a map of the area so that the whole team has an agreed understanding of the actual shape of the geographical entity. Furthermore, the focus of the Rapid Appraisal must be clarified, and be consistent with the WHO definition of health, Rapid Appraisal tends to look at the totality of need rather than focusing on specific client groups or specific problem areas.

In most cases data already exist which are relevant to the community selected. This can be systematic data which can be found at central locations, such as census or activity data; it can also be anecdotal data, collected for specific purposes, and which is not readily available, such as reports by

Day one

9.00–10.30	Objectives of the workshop and the RA project. What is a Rapid Appraisal?
10.30–10.45	Break.
10.45–11.15	Defining the area and focus.
11.15–12.15	Defining and analysing existing data.
12.15–1.15	Break.
1.15–3.15	Generating the questions within the information profile. Small group work.
3.15–3.30	Break.
3.30–4.00	Small group work continued.
4.00–5.00	Constructing the interview schedule.

Day two

9.00–10.00	Constructing the interview schedule continued.
10.00–10.30	Using the interview schedule. Small group work.
10.30–10.45	Break.
10.45–11.15	Small group work continued.
11.15–12.15	Generating the list of respondents.
12.15–1.00	Break.
1.00–1.30	Small team formation.
1.30–3.00	Defining the work programme and timetables.

Figure 9.1 Rapid Appraisal workshop.

voluntary organizations, projects carried out by professionals studying for further qualifications and so on. Making an inventory of all possible data sources, and deciding upon criteria for inclusion in the Rapid Appraisal is the first step in the collection of secondary data, and defines the framework for analysis. At this stage the responsibilities for collecting and analysing specific data sets are divided among team members.

On the basis of the information profile (see Figure 2.1, p.24) questions have to be generated within each category of the profile and which are locally relevant. This exercise is carried out in the workshop through a series of 'brainstorms' whereby team members formulate questions for each category, which are then reduced to three or four key questions. The brainstorms are important for the team in that they clarify their thinking about community concerns, and focus on the central issues through the process of reduction. When the interview schedule is finalized, team members have to trial the appropriateness and workability of the schedule in mock interviews with each other. This helps to iron out ambiguities in the schedule or its administration.

It is often useful to have a few team members who know the chosen community well, so that a list of people who should be interviewed can be drafted. Generally, three lists are constructed: one for community leaders, one for people at the centre of social networks, and one for people who work in the community. If at all possible the lists should contain equal numbers, and the total listing should be around 30 people. This allows for the 'snowballing' of the sample, with a final sample size of approximately 50 respondents (groups count as one respondent).

The larger Rapid Appraisal team is then subdivided into three or four smaller teams, each containing people from different organizations and/or disciplines in order to maximize the triangulation effect within the interviews. Each subteam agrees a timetable for interviews which will have to fit within the overall work schedule and target date for final delivery of the report and other feedback mechanisms.

STEP 4. FIELDWORK

An agreed period of fieldwork allows individuals to collate their secondary data, and to carry out interviews in their subteams. For the interviews it is considered good practice to contact possible community respondents through individuals known to them who can provide an explanation about the purpose and format of a Rapid Appraisal interview. Consent can be obtained through this source, and then the subteam can arrange a time and place for the interview. Written backup material, outlining the purpose, process and feedback mechanisms, is useful to produce and can be given to respondents prior to the interviews.

For the interview itself most teams adopt a division of labour with one person interviewing and the other team member(s) making notes. The interviews must be carried out in a relaxed atmosphere, and therefore, the respondent should choose the site. The application of the semi-structured format assists in allowing the respondent to determine the content with the interviewer gently guiding through the various themes. The interviewer has to ensure that the interviewee speaks for the subset of the community on which the interview focuses, rather than reflecting the respondent's personal perspective.

During the interview the other member(s) of the interview team take notes (verbatim where necessary). After the interview the notes and impressions are compared in order to arrive at a common understanding of the issues raised in the interview. Any observations about the environment, social context or any other relevant issues are noted and shared. At the end of the round of interviews each subteam makes a preliminary analysis of the data they have collected to present at the meeting of the full team.

STEP 5. GENERATING A NEEDS LIST

In a workshop (often half a day is sufficient) the subteams come together to share their experiences and their preliminary data analyses. The information profile acts as an organizing device for the analysis of all the data, that is, observations, secondary data and interviews. Through discussion all the data on each category is reduced to a number of statements describing key needs in the community. The number can vary from three to eight. It is important to agree on a maximum number because prioritizing more than eight needs will be very difficult to do. Sometimes, needs lists from different categories are combined, for example, community composition, community organization and community capacity. Also, in some Rapid Appraisals the category health and social policy has not generated a needs list.

STEP 6. PRIORITIZATION OF NEEDS

The needs lists have to be presented to the respondents so they can decide on their priorities within the different categories. At this stage the team can broaden out the process and adopt a number of strategies to secure more extensive community involvement. For example, they can include people from specific interest groups in the community, take a random sample of the community or create *ad hoc* groups for prioritization discussions. The possibilities are endless, and depend on resources and time constraints, and, of course, on the way in which community involvement is defined.

It is necessary beforehand to have an agreed procedure for analysing the priorities and choices that have to be made between different scoring methods and statistical or weighted analysis. Teams have to decide on how they explain this approach to the people they ask to be involved in the priority-setting exercise, and they also have to explain the feedback and implementation process. Making choices about the priority-setting depends on a number of factors, such as resources, time, community preferences, the breadth and depth required and so on. As a minimum most Rapid Appraisals include the respondents from the first phase in the priority-setting exercise; in others this is expanded to include key individuals or community groups, or focus groups are set up to debate the needs lists.

The analysis of the priorities can be carried out by one or two team members, depending on the skills available. If a statistical analysis is adopted it is advisable to ask for appropriate advice. The outcome of this stage should be a clear listing, in priority order, of needs within each category. Depending on the level of refinement distinctions can be made between and within respondent groupings (see Chapter 5).

STEP 7. FEEDBACK

There is no set approach to offering feedback to the respondents and the community at large. The only rule is that meaningful feedback has to be given, both about the process and outcome in order to make the Rapid Appraisal transparent, and to be accountable for the results of the exercise and its recommendations.

In most Rapid Appraisals a report has been written about the process and the priority listings. This can be accompanied by a short summary or letter to be distributed to the whole community and backed-up by an article in the local newspaper or a feature on the local radio. Public meetings have been used to discuss the findings or through smaller meetings with specific groups such as ethnic minority interest groups, people with disabilities or resident associations. Again, the range of possibilities is endless, and depends very much on the level of local interest and organizational structures.

STEP 8. PROGRAMME OF CHANGE

The feedback process is often directly tied into the programme of change, especially when the medium of public meetings is used. Through these meetings discussions can take place between the Rapid Appraisal team and community groups about translating findings into action. In many Rapid Appraisals a small number of actions are agreed which can be achieved within a short time (usually six months) with clearly defined objectives, which involve both the community and one (or more) agencies and which are at or near the top of the priority listing. Some key priorities cannot be addressed because they are too large scale, are beyond the scope of the organizations involved, take too much time, and so on. Agreement has to be reached about the timing and order of priority actions, the way in which they are planned and carried out, and the involvement of individuals, groups and organizations. A clear division of labour also has to be agreed upon.

Some action plans are aimed at the community as a whole, others are for the benefit of particular groupings. It is advisable to find an acceptable balance between general and specific actions in order to maintain credibility with the community, and explicitly discuss the reasons behind the selection.

STEP 9. EVALUATION

As the action plans all operate within a limited time frame, regular evaluation of progress is possible. A mechanism has to be found or devised to carry out such evaluations, which can be through established community groups or a specially created Rapid Appraisal implementation group. Agreement has to be reached about the criteria for success, and the way in which certain actions are brought to a close. Furthermore, there has to be an accepted approach to moving new priorities 'up the ladder', and perhaps redefining priorities in the light of achievements on earlier priorities. It is essential to involve the community in the evaluation and re-ordering of priorities so that a sustained programme of action can be instigated and supported by both the community and relevant organizations.

STEP 10. FURTHER WORK

A Rapid Appraisal has a limited shelf life, and after a few years it is likely that a community has evolved as a result of wider social and economic changes, or partly as a result of the earlier Rapid Appraisal work. A number of options are open, including doing a new Rapid Appraisal or developing different initiatives such as visioning or incorporating community involvement in organizational structures. The way a Rapid Appraisal is taken forward in the long term depends both on local circumstances and the broader policy context.

References

Abel-Smith, B. (1994) *An introduction to health. Policy, planning and financing,* Longman, London and New York.

Adler, P. and Adler, P. (1994) Observational techniques, in *Handbook of qualitative research* (eds N. Denzin and Y. Lincoln), Sage, Thousand Oaks, pp. 377–92.

Alderslade, R. and Hunter, D. (1994) Commissioning and public health, *Journal of Management in Medicine,* 8 (6), 20–31.

Annett, H. and Rifkin, S. (1988) *Improving urban health,* World Health Organization, Geneva.

Arnstein, S. (1969) A ladder of citizen participation, *The American Journal of Planners,* 35 (4), 216–24.

Ashton, J. and Seymour, H. (1988) *The new public health,* Open University Press, Milton Keynes.

Atkinson, P. (1990) *The ethnographic imagination: textual constructions of reality,* Routledge, London.

Baker, M. (1991) *Research for marketing*, MacMillan, Houndsmill, Basingstoke.

Barrett, S. and McMahon, L. (1990) Public management in uncertainty: a micro-political perspective of the health service in the United Kingdom, *Policy and Politics*, 18 (4), 257–68.

Becker, H. (1961) *Boys in white: student culture in medical school*, Chicago University Press, Chicago.

Bell, C. and Encel, S. (1978) Introduction, in *Inside the whale* (eds C. Bell and S. Encel), Pergamon Press, Oxford, pp.1–13.

Bezold, C. (1994) Visioning workshop, *International Health Futures Network Conference, Healthcare 2000,* 25–28 May, 1994, Utrecht.

Bezold, C. and Hancock, T. (1993) An overview of the health futures field for the WHO health futures consultation, in *Health futures in support of health for all* (A. Taket), WHO, Geneva.

Bezold, C., Corr, C. and Morrison, R. (1993) *21st Century health systems: principles and visions,* Celebration Health and the International Health Futures Network, Florida.

Bibeau, G. (1988) A step towards thick thinking: from webs of significance to connections across dimensions, *Medical Anthropology Quarterly,* 2, 402–16.

Black, D. (1993) Deprivation and health, *British Medical Journal*, 307, 1630–1.

Boaden, M., Cropper, S. and Ong, B. N. (1995) *Clinicians' involvement in business planning,* British Association of Medical Managers, Stockport.

Boezeman, J. (1986) Scenarios in Shell, *Scenarios and other methods to support long term health planning. Theory and practice* (eds J. Brouwer and R. Schreuder), STG (Steering Committee on Future Health Scenarios), Noordwijk.

Bowling, A., Jacobson, B. and Southgate, L. (1993) Exploration in consultation of the public and health professionals on priority setting in an inner London health district, *Social Science and Medicine,* 37 (7), 851–7.

Bradshaw, J. (1972) A taxonomy of social need, in *Problems and progress in medical care,* (ed. G. Mclachlan), Nuffield Provincial Hospitals Trust, Oxford, pp.71–82.

Bradshaw, J. (1994) The conceptualization and measurement of need: a social policy perspective, in *Researching the people's health,* (eds J. Popay and G. Williams), Routledge, London, pp.45–57.

Brannen, J. (1992) *Mixing methods: qualitative and quantitative research,* Avebury, Aldershot.

Brazier, J., Harper, R., Jones, N. *et al.* (1992) Validating the SF-36 health survey questionnaire: a new outcome measure for primary care, *British Medical Journal,* 305, 160–4.

Brewer, J. and Hunter, A. (1989) *Multimethod research. A synthesis of styles,* Sage, London.

Briggs, C. (1986) *Learning how to ask: a sociological appraisal of the interview in social science research,* Cambridge University Press, Cambridge.

Bulmer, M. (1987) *The social basis of community care,* Allen and Unwin, London.

Calman, K. (1994) The profession of medicine, *British Medical Journal*, 309, 1140–3.

Calnan, M. (1995) Citizens' views on health care, *Journal of Management in Medicine,* 9, 4, 17–23.

Carr-Hill, R. (1991) Allocating resources to health care: is the QALY(Quality Adjusted Life Year) a technical solution to a political problem?, *International Journal of Health Services,* 21 (2), 351–63.

Cernea, M. (1992) Re-tooling in applied social investigation for development planning: some methodological issues in rapid assessment procedures, In *RAP: rapid assessment procedures: qualitative methodologies for planning and evaluation of health related programs* (eds S. Scrimshaw and D. Gleason), International Nutrition Foundation for Developing Countries, Boston, pp.11–23.

Chambers, R. (1992) Actual or potential uses of RRA/PRA methods in health and nutrition, *Rapid Rural Appraisal Notes,* 16, 101–10.

Cicourel, A. (1982) Interviews, surveys and the problem of ecological validity, *American Sociologist,* 17, 11–20.

Colombani, P de., Borrini, M., Meira de Melo, M. and Irshaid, M. (1992) Exploring the potential for primary environmental care: Rapid Appraisal in squatter communities, *Rapid Rural Appraisal Notes,* 16, 88–100.

Comaroff, J. and Maguire, P. (1981) Ambiguity and the search for meaning: childhood leukemia in the modern clinical context, *Social Science and Medicine,* 15B, 115–23.

Conway, G. (1988) Editorial, *Rapid Rural Appraisal Notes,* Institute for Environment and Development, 1, 3.

Cooper, D. (1994) Productive, relational and ubiquitous: conceptualising power within Foucauldian feminism, *Sociology,* 28 (2), 435–54.

Cornwall, A. (1992) Body mapping in Health RRA/PRA, *Rapid Rural Appraisal Notes,* 16, 69–76.

Cox, B. *et al.* (1993) *The health and lifestyle survey: seven years on,* Aldershot, Dartmouth.

Crawhaw, R., Garland, M., Hines, B. and Anderson, B. (1990) Developing principles for prudent health care allocation. The continuing Oregon experiment, *The Western Journal of Medicine,* 152 (4), 441–6.

Croft, S. and Beresford, P. (1992) The politics of participation, *Critical Social Policy,* 35, 20–43.

Crow, G. and Allen, G. (1994) *Community life. An introduction to local social relations,* Harvester Wheatsheaf, Brighton.

Culver, C. and Gert, B. (1982) *Philosophy and medicine,* Oxford University Press, Oxford.

Dale, A., Arber, S. and Procter, M. (1988) *Doing secondary analysis,* Unwin Hyman, London.

Dalley, G. (1988) *Ideologies of caring. Rethinking community and collectivism,* MacMillan, Basingstoke and London.

Daniels, N. (1991) Is the Oregon rationing plan fair? *Journal of the American Medical Association,* 265 (17), 2232–5.

Denzin, N. (1978) *The research act: a theoretical introduction to sociological methods,* 2nd edn, McGraw-Hill, New York.

Denzin, N. and Lincoln, Y. (eds)(1994) *Handbook of Qualitative Research,* Sage, Thousand Oaks.

Department of Health (1992) *The health of the nation. A strategy for health in England,* HMSO, Cmd 1986, London.

Desai, M. (1986) Drawing the line: on defining the poverty threshold, in *Excluding the poor,* (ed. P. Golding), CPAG, London.

Dixon, J. and Welch, G. (1991) Priority setting: lessons from Oregon, *Lancet,* 337, 891–4.

Donaldson, C. (1989) Programme-specific QALYs: a reply, *Journal of Health Economics,* 8, 489–91

Donaldson, C., Atkinson, A. and Bond, J. *et al.* (1988). Should QALYs be programme specific?*Journal of Health Economics,* 7, 239–57.

Donovan, J. and Coast, J. (1994) Public preferences in priority setting – unresolved issues, in *Setting priorities in health care* (ed. M. Malek), John Wiley and Sons, London, pp.31–43.

Doyal, L. (1993) Thinking about human need, *New Left Review,* 201, 113–28.

Doyal, L. and Gough, I. (1991) *A theory of human need,* MacMillan, London.

Dunning, A. (1992) *Choices in Health Care,* A report by the Government Committee on Choices in Health Care, Zoetermeer, The Netherlands.

DYG Inc. (1994) *What creates health? Individuals and communities respond,* The Healthcare Forum, San Francisco.

Eddy, D. (1991) What's going on in Oregon? *Journal of the American Medical Association,* 266 (3), 417–20.

Eden, C. (1989) Operational research as negotiation,in *Operational research and the social sciences* (eds M. Jackson, P. Keys and S. Cropper), Plenum Press, New York and London, pp.43–50.

Eisenberg, L. (1977) Disease and illness: distinctions between professional and popular ideas of sickness, *Culture, medicine and psychiatry,* 1, 19–23.

Fazey, C. (1987) *Evaluating drug dependency clinics: theoretical frameworks and methodological considerations,* Studies of drug issues: Report 1, Centre for Urban Studies, Liverpool.

Federation of Swedish County Councils (1992) *Crossroads. Future options for Swedish health care,* Stockholm.

Finch, J. (1989) *Family obligations and social change,* Polity Press in association with Blackwell, Oxford.

Fink, A. (1993) *Evaluation fundamentals. Guiding health programs, research and policy,* Sage, Newbury Park.

Flynn, R. (1992) *Structures of control in health management,* Routledge, London.

Foddy, W. (1993) *Constructing questions for interviews and questionnaires. Theory and practice in social research,* Cambridge University Press, Cambridge.

Fontana, A. and Frey, J. (1994) Interviewing. The art of science, in *Handbook of qualitative research,* (eds N.Denzin and Y. Lincoln), Sage, Thousand Oaks, pp.361–76.

Foucault, M. (1973) *The birth of the clinic: an archaeology of medical perception,* Pantheon, New York.

Foucault, M. (1978) *The history of sexuality: an introduction,* Penguin, Harmondsworth.

Freidson, E. (1970) *Profession of medicine: a study of the sociology of applied knowledge,* Dodd Mead, New York.

Freidson, E. (1988) *Profession of medicine: a study of the sociology of applied knowledge, with a new afterword,* University of Chicago Press, Chicago.

Freire, P. (1973) *Pedagogy of the oppressed,* Penguin, London.

Garrard, E. (1994) *Conceptions of health: a philosophical approach,* Seminar given at the Centre for Health Planning and Management, Keele University, Keele, January.

GCL and HSMU (1992) *Caring for the community in the 21st century. Integrated purchasing of public services. A discussion paper,* Macclesfield and Manchester.

Gibson, T. (1994) Showing what you mean (not just talking about it), *Rapid Rural Appraisal Notes,* 21, 41–8.

Gillon, R. (1986) *Philosophical medical ethics,* John Wiley and Sons, Chichester, on behalf of the *British Medical Journal.*

Glaser, B. and Strauss, A. (1967) *The discovery of grounded theory. Strategies for qualitative research,* Aldine, Chicago.

Green, A. and Barker, C. (1988) Priority setting and economic appraisal: whose priorities – the community or the economist?, *Social Science and Medicine,* 26 (9), 919–29.

Griffiths, R. (1983) *NHS Management Inquiry,* Report, DHSS, London.

Gudex, C. and Kind, P. (1987) *The QALY Toolkit,* Discussion paper 76, Centre for Health Economics, University of York, York.

Hadorn, D. (1991) Setting health care priorities in Oregon. Cost-effectiveness meets the rule of rescue, *Journal of the American Medical Association,* 265 (17), 2218–25.

Hakim, C. (1987) *Research design. Strategies and choices in the design of social research*, Allen and Unwin, London.

Ham, C. (1993a) *Europe. Future health care options,* Institute of Health Services Management, London.

Ham, C. (1993b) Priority setting in the health services: lessons from experience, in *Rationing of health and social care*, (ed. I. Allen), Policy Studies Institute, London, pp.1–7.

Ham, C. (1994) *Management and competition in the new NHS,* Radcliffe Medical Press, Oxford.

Hare, R. (1986) Health, *Journal of Medical Ethics,* 12, 174–81.

Hart, E. and Bond, M. (1995) *Action research for health and social care. A guide to practice,* Open University Press, Buckingham.

Harrison, S. and Hunter, D. (1994) *Rationing health care,* Institute for Public Policy Research, London.

Harrison, S., Hunter, D., Marnoch, G. and Pollitt, C. (1992) *Just managing: power and culture in the National Health Service,* MacMillan, London.

Hawker, M. (1989) Consumer participation as community development: action in an ambiguous context, *Community Development Journal,* 24 (4), 283–91.

Helman, C. (1985) *Culture, health and illness*, Wright, Bristol.

Hewitt, M. (1993) Social movements and social need: problems with postmodern political theory, *Critical Social Policy,* 37, 52–74.

Hildebrandt, E. (1994) A model for community involvement in health (CIH) program development, *Social Science and Medicine,* 39 (2), 247–54.

Hillery, G. (1955) Definitions of community: areas of agreement, *Rural Sociology,* 80 (2), 111–23.

Hopkins, A. and Maxwell, R. (1990) Contracts and quality of care, *British Medical Journal,* 300, 919–22.

Hopton, J. and Dlugolecka, M. (1995) Patients' perceptions of need for primary health care services: useful for priority setting?, *British Medical Journal,* 310, 1237–40.

Hugman, R. (1991) *Power in caring professions,* MacMillan, London.

Hunter, D. (1991) Managing medicine: a response to the 'crisis'. *Social Science and Medicine.* 32, (4), 44–9

Hunter, D. (1994) Social research and health policy in the aftermath of the NHS reforms, in *Researching the people's health* (eds. J Popay and G. Williams), Routledge, London, pp. 15–31.

Hurtado, E. (ed.) (1990) *Rapid anthropological procedures for community-based assessment and analysis: making it rapid, responsive and relevant,* Community Nutrition Research, IDRC, Canada.

Illich, I. (1975) *Medical nemesis*, Calder and Boyars, London.

Illsley, R. and LeGrand, J. (1987) *Measurement and inequality in health*, Welfare State Programme Discussion Paper 12, London School of Economics, London.

Jack, R. (1983) Victorian vices, *Community Care,* November 10, 15–6.

Jamous, H. and Peloille, B. (1970) Professions or self-perpetuating systems? Changes in the French university-hospital system, in *Professions and professionalization* (ed. J. Jackson), Cambridge University Press, Cambridge.

Janesick, V. (1994) The dance of qualitative research, in *Handbook of qualitative research*, (eds N. Denzin and Y. Lincoln), Sage, Thousand Oaks, pp.209–19.

Joule, N. (1993) Involving users of health care services: moving beyond lip service, *Quality in Health Care*, 2, 211–2.

Kelleher, D. (1994) Self-help groups and their relationship to medicine, in *Challenging medicine*, (eds J. Gabe, D. Kelleher, and G. Williams), Routledge, London, pp. 104–17.

Kelleher, D., Gabe, J. and Williams, G. (1994) Understanding medical dominance in the modern world, in *Challenging medicine*, (eds J. Gabe, D. Kelleher and G. Williams), Routledge, London, pp.xi–xxix.

Kind, P., Rosser, R. and Williams, A. (1982) Valuation of quality of life: some psycho-metric evidence, in *The value of life and safety* (ed. M. Jones-Lee), North Holland Publishing Company, The Netherlands.

Klein, R. and Redmayne, S. (1992) *Patterns of research priorities*, National Association of Health Authorities and Trusts, Birmingham.

Krueger, R. (1994) *Focus groups*, 2nd edn, Sage, London.

Kuhn, T. (1970) *The structure of scientific revolutions*, International Encyclopedia of Unified Science, 2, 2, University of Chicago Press, Chicago.

Kumar, K. (1994) An overview of Rapid Appraisal methods in development settings, in *Rapid Appraisal methods*, (ed. K. Kumar), The World Bank, Washington, pp.8–22.

Larson, M. Sarfatti (1977) *The rise of professionalism*, University of California Press, Berkeley.

Last, M. (ed.) (1988) *A dictionary of epidemiology*, Oxford University Press, Oxford.

Lilford, R. and Harrison, S. (1994) Health services research – what it is, how to do it, and why it matters, *Health Services Management Research*, 7 (4), 214–9.

Locker, D. (1981) *Symptoms and illness*, Tavistock, London.

Lukes, S. (1974) *Power: a radical view*, MacMillan, London.

MacDonald, J. (1993) *Primary health care, Medicine in its place*, Erathscan, London.

MacGregor, D. (1960) *The human side of enterprise*, McGraw–Hill, New York.

McKeown, T. (1976) *The role of medicine: dream, mirage or nemesis?* Nuffield Provincial Hospitals Trust, London.

McKeown, K., Whitelaw, S., Hambleton, D. and Green, F. (1994) Setting priorities – science, art or politics, in *Setting priorities in health care*, (ed. M. Malek), John Wiley and Sons, London, pp.19–29.

McNerney, W. (1992) Introduction to *The Belmont Vision for health care in America*, A project of the Institute of Alternative Futures, Alexandria, Virginia, pp.11–3.

Marsden, D. and Oakley, P. (1991) Future issues and perspectives in the evaluation of social development, *Community Development Journal*, 26 (4), 314–28.

Marsden, D., Oakley, P. and Pratt, B. (1994) *Measuring the process: guidelines for evaluating social development*, Intrac Publications, Oxford.

Mawhinney, B. (1994) *Purchasing for health: involving local people*, Speech for the National Purchasing Conference, Birmingham, April 13.

May, A. (ed.) (1994) *Health Care in Europe*, Health Service Journal publication, London.

Maynard, A. (1994) Prioritising health care – dreams and reality, in *Setting priorities in health care,* (ed. M. Malek), John Wiley and Sons, London, pp.1–18.

Mayo, M. (1994) *Communities and Caring,* MacMillan, Basingstoke and London.

Maxwell, R. (1984) Quality assessment in health, *British Medical Journal,* Vol.288, May 12, 1470–2.

Miles, M. and Huberman, A. (1994) *Qualitative data analysis. An expanded sourcebook,* 2nd edn, Sage, Thousand Oaks.

Moustakas, C. (1994) *Phenomenological research methods,* Sage, Thousand Oaks.

Munslow, B., Fitzgerald, P. and McLennan, A. (1995) Introduction. Sustainable development: turning vision into reality, in *Managing sustainable development in South Africa,* (eds B. Munslow, P. Fitzgerald and A. McLennan), Oxford University Press, Capetown, pp.v-xxxix.

Navarro, V. (1978) *Class struggle, the State and medicine: a historical and contemporary analysis of the medical sector in Great Britain,* M. Robinson, London.

National Council for Voluntary Organisations (1991) *Changing the balance. Power and people who use services,* NCVO Community Care Project, London.

National Health Service Management Executive (1990) *Assessing health care need,* DHA Project Paper, June, London.

National Health Service Management Executive (1992) *Local Voices. The views of local people in purchasing for health,* NHSME, London.

Newby, H. (1987) Community and urban life, in *The new introducing sociology,* (ed. P. Worsley), Penguin, Harmondsworth, pp. 238–72.

Nicolson, M. and McLaughlin, C. (1987) Social constructionism and medical sociology: a reply to M. R. Bury, *Sociology of Health and Illness,* 9 (2), 107–26.

Oakley, A. (1980) *Women confined,* Martin Robertson, Oxford.

Oakley, A. (1981) Interviewing women: a contradiction in terms, in *Doing feminist research,* (ed. H. Roberts), Routledge and Kegan Paul, London, pp.31–61.

Oakley, P. (1989) *Community involvement in health development,* World Health Organization, Geneva.

Ong, B. N. (1986) Women in the transition to socialism in Sub-Saharan Africa, in *Africa's problems in the transition to socialism,* (ed. B. Munslow), Zed Books, London, pp.72–94.

Ong, B. N. (1993) *The practice of health services research,* Chapman and Hall, London.

Parker, G. (1990) *With due care and attention. A review of research on informal care,* Family Policy Studies Centre, London.

Parker, G. (1993) *With this body: caring and disability in marriage,* Open University Press, Buckingham.

Parston, G. (1993) Caring, sharing managers, *Health Service Journal,* 10 June, 23.

Paton, C. (1993) *Competition and planning in the NHS,* Chapman and Hall, London.

Paton, C. (1995) Contriving competition, *Health Services Journal,* March 30, 30–1.

Pettigrew, A., McKee, L. and Ferlie, E. (1992) *Shaping strategic change,* Sage, London.

Peters, T. and Waterman, R. (1982) *In search of excellence,* Harper & Row, New York.

Pfeffer, N. and Pollock, A. (1993a) Doors of perception, *Health Services Journal,* 2 September, 26.

Pfeffer, N. and Pollock, A. (1993b) Public opinion and the NHS. The unaccountable in pursuit of the uninformed, *British Medical Journal,* 307, 750–1.

Phillips, D. (1971) *Knowledge from what: theories and methods in social research,* Rand McNally, Chicago.

Plummer, K. (1988) Organising AIDS, in *Social aspects of AIDS* (eds P. Aggleton and H. Homans.), Falmer Press, Barcombe, pp.20–52.

Pollock, A. (1992) Local voices. The bankruptcy of the democratic process, *British Medical Journal*, 305, 535–6.

Pope, C. and Mays, N. (1993) Opening the black box: an encounter in the corridors of health services research, *British Medical Journal*, 306, 315–8.

Pope, C. and Mays, N. (1995) Reaching the parts other methods cannot reach: an introduction to qualitative methods in health and health services research, *British Medical Journal*, 311, 42–5, (first article in a series of seven).

Poullier, J-P. (1994) *Unfinished health care reforms: the lessons,* Paper delivered at the European Health Policy Forum, Leuven, 8–9 December.

Research Unit in Health and Behavioural Change (1989) *Changing the public health,* John Wiley & Sons, Chichester.

Richman, J. (1987) *Medicine and health,* Longman, London.

Rifkin, S. (1990) *Community participation in maternal and child health/family planning programmes,* World Health Organization, Geneva.

Rifkin, S. (1992) Rapid Appraisals for health: an overview, *Rapid Rural Appraisal Notes*, 16, 7–12.

Rifkin. S., Muller. F. and Bichmann. W. (1988) Primary Health Care: on measuring participation, *Social Science and Medicine*, 26 (9), 931–40.

Rifkin, S. and Walt, G. (1986) Why health improves: defining the issues concerning 'Comprehensive Primary Health Care' and 'Selective Primary Health Care', *Social Science and Medicine*, 23, (6), 559–66

Riley, C., Warner, M., Pullen, A. and Semple Piggot, C. (eds) (1995) *Releasing resources to achieve health gain,* Radcliffe Medical Press, Oxford and New York.

Roethlisberger, F. and Dickson, W. (1939) *Management and the worker*, Harvard University Press, Cambridge.

Rosener, J. (1990) Ways women lead, *Harvard Business Review,* 119–25.

Rossman, G. and Wilson, B. (1984) Numbers and words: combining quantitative and qualitative methods in a single large-scale evaluation study, *Evaluation Review*, 9 (5), 627–43.

Rossman, G. and Wilson, B. (1991) Numbers and words revisited: being 'shamelessly eclectic', *Evaluation* Review, 16.

St. Leger, S., Schnieden, H. and Walsworth-Bell, J. (1992) *Evaluating health services' effectiveness,* Open University Press, Milton Keynes.

Saltman, R. (1992) *Patient choice and patient empowerment: a conceptual analysis,* Swedish Center for Policy and Business Studies, Occasional Paper, no.4, Stockholm.

Scrimshaw, S. and Gleason, D. (eds) (1992) *RAP: rapid assessment procedures: qualitative methodologies for planning and evaluation of health related programs,* International Nutrition Foundation for Developing Countries, Boston.

Sen, G. and Grown, C. (1988) *Development, crises and alternative visions,* Earthscan, London.

Senge, P. (1992) *The fifth discipline: art and practice of the learning organization,* Century Business, London.

Siegel, S. and Castellan, N. (1988) *Nonparametric statistics for behavioural sciences,* 2nd edn, McGraw Hill, New York.

Sloggett, A and Joshi, H. (1994) Higher mortality in deprived areas: community or personal disadvantage? *British Medical Journal,* 309, 1470–4.

Smith, R. (1994) Medicine's core values, *British Medical Journal,* 309, 1248–49.

Snee, K. (1991) *Dallam on health,* Warrington.

Soper, K. (1993) Review: A theory of human need, *New Left Review,* 197, 113–28.

Spradley, J. (1979) *The ethnographic interview,* Holt, Rhinehart and Winston, New York.

Stacey, M. (1988) *The sociology of health and healing,* Unwin Hyman, London.

Steering Committee on Future Health Scenarios (1992) *Chronic diseases in the year 2005,* Vol.2, Kluwer Academic Publishers, Enschede.

Stevens, A. and Raftery, J. (eds) (1994) *Health care needs assessment. The epidemiologically based needs assessment reviews, Vol.1 and Vol.2.,* Radcliffe Medical Press, Oxford and New York.

Stewart, D. and Shamdasani, P. (1990) *Focus Groups. Theory and practice,* Sage, London.

Stocking, B. (1984) *Initiative and inertia: case studies in the NHS,* Nuffield Provincial Hospitals Trust, London.

Stocking, B., Jennett, B. and Spiby, J. (1991) *Criteria for change. The history and impact of consensus development conferences in the UK,* King's Fund Centre, London.

Strong, P. and Robinson, J. (1990) *The NHS under new management,* Open University Press, Milton Keynes.

Sykes, W., Collins, M., Hunter, D. *et al.* (1992) *Listening to local voices,* Nuffield Institute for Health Services Studies and Public Health Research and Resource Centre, Leeds and Salford.

Taket, A. (1993) *Health futures in support of health for all,* Report of an international consultation convened by the World Health Organization, Geneva, 19–23 July, 1993, WHO, Geneva.

Taussig, M. (1980) Reifcation and the consiousness of the patient, *Social Science and Medicine,* 14B, 3–13

Tomorrow's doctoring. Patient, heal thyself (1995), *the Economist,* 4 February, 19–21.

Townsend, P. (1979) *Poverty in the United Kingdom,* Penguin, Harmondsworth.

Townsend, P. and Davidson, N. (1982) *Inequalities in health: the Black report,* Penguin, Harmondsworth.

Upton, C. and Taylor, P. (1995) Coming in from the cold, *Health Service Journal,* 16 March, 22–4.

Vågerö, D. (1995) Health inequalities as policy issues – reflections on ethics, policy and public health, *Sociology of Health and Illness,* 17(1), 1–11.

Van der Geest, J., Speckmann, J. and Streefland, P. (1990) Primary Health Care in a multi-level perspective: towards a research agenda, *Social Science and Medicine,* 30 (9), 1025–34.

Van Maanen, J. (1979) The fact of fiction in organizational ethnography, *Administrative Science Quarterly,* 24, 539–611.

Walt, G. (1994) *Health Policy: an introduction to process and power,* Zed Books and Witwatersrand University Press, London and Johannesburg.

Warner, M., Pugh, S., Riley, C. and Rhodes, J. (1993) *Blurring the boundaries – the future of hospital and primary care. The case of gastrointestinal disease,* Welsh Health Planning Forum and Department of Medicine, University College of Wales, Cardiff.

Welbourn, A. (1991) RRA and the analysis of difference, *Rapid Rural Appraisal Notes,* 14, 14–23.

Welbourn, A. (1992) A note on the use of disease problem ranking with relation to socio-economic well-being: an example from Sierra Leone, *Rapid Rural Appraisal Notes,* 16, 86–7.

Wellman, B. (1979) The community question: the intimate network of East Yorkers, *American Journal of Sociology,* 84 (5), 1201–31.

Welsh Office (1989) *Strategic intent and direction for the NHS in Wales,* NHS Directorate, Welsh Health Planning Forum, Cardiff.

Welsh Office NHS Directorate (1992) *Caring for the future. The pathfinder,* Cardiff.

Wertheimer, A. (1991) *A chance to speak out. Consulting service users and carers about community care,* King's Fund Centre, London.

Whitehead, M. (1992) *The health divide,* 2nd edn, Penguin, Harmondsworth.

Williams, A. (1985) Economics of coronary artery bypass grafting, *British Medical Journal,* 291, 326–9.

Williams, A. (1988) Priority setting in public and private health care. A guide through the ideological jungle, *Journal of Health Economics,* 7, 173–83.

Williams, A. (1989) Comment: Should QALYs be programme specific?, *Journal of Health Economics,* 8, 485–7.

Williams, A. (1992) Cost-effectiveness analysis: is it ethical?, *Journal of Medical Ethics,* 18, 7–11.

Williams, F. (1992) Somewhere over the rainbow: universality and diversity in social policy, in *Social Policy Review* (eds N. Manning and R. Page), Social Policy Association, pp.200–19.

Williams, G. and Popay, J. (1994a) Lay knowledge and the privilege of experience, in *Challenging medicine* (eds J. Gabe, D. Kelleher and G. Williams), Routledge, London, pp.118–39.

Williams, G. and Popay, J. (1994b) Researching the people's health: dilemmas and opportunities for social scientists, in *Researching the people's health* (eds J. Popay and G. Williams), Routledge, London, pp.99–114.

Williams, R. (1976) *Keywords. A vocabulary of culture and society,* Fontana, London.

Wistow, G. (1995) Coming apart at the seams, *Health Service Journal,* 2 March, 24–5.

World Commission on Environment and Development (1987) *Our common future,* Oxford University Press, Oxford, pp.43–65.

World Health Organization (1981) *Global Strategy for Health for All by the year 2000,* WHO, Geneva.

World Health Organization (1985) *Targets for Health for All,* WHO Regional Office for Europe, Copenhagen.

World Health Organization (1988a) *From Alma-Ata to the year 2000,* WHO, Geneva.

World Health Organization (1988b) *Ecological models for Healthy Cities planning,* Report on WHO workshop, Liverpool, 25–27 March, Rapporteur P.Flynn, WHO, Copenhagen.

World Health Organization (1989) *European Charter on environment and health*, WHO, Copenhagen.

World Health Organization (1992) *A call for new public health action. Report of the Saitama Public Health Summit,* Omiya city, Saitama prefecture, Japan, WHO, Geneva.

World Health Organization (1993) *Implementation of the global strategy for Health for All by the Year 2000: second evaluation,* Eighth report on the world health situation, Vol.1, Global Review, WHO, Geneva.

World Health Organization/UNICEF (1978) *Primary Health Care: the Alma Ata conference,* WHO, Geneva.

Worsley, P. (1982) Non-western medical systems, *Annual Review of Anthropology,* 11, 315–48.

Yeo, E. and Yeo, S. (1988) On the use of community in *New Views of Co-operation* (ed. S. Yeo), Routledge, London.

Index